USDA

United States
Department of
Agriculture

Forest Service

General Technical
Report NC-260

Technical Guide

2006

Conservation Assessments for Five Forest Bat Species in the Eastern United States

Edited by
Frank R. Thompson, III

Thompson, Frank R., III, ed. 2006. Conservation assessments for five forest bat species in the Eastern United States. Gen. Tech. Rep. NC-260. St. Paul, MN: U.S. Department of Agriculture, Forest Service, North Central Research Station. 82 p.

Assesses the status, distribution, conservation, and management considerations for five Regional Forester Sensitive Species of forest bats on national forests in the Eastern United States: eastern pipistrelle, evening bat, southeastern myotis, eastern small-footed myotis, and northern long-eared bat. Includes information on the taxonomy, description, life history, habitat distribution, status, and population biology of each species.

KEY WORDS: conservation status, habitat use, life history, *Myotis austroriparius* (southeastern myotis), *Myotis leibii* (eastern small-footed myotis), *Myotis septentrionalis* (northern long-eared bat), *Pipistrellus subflavus* (eastern pipistrelle), *Nycticeius humeralis* (evening bat), Region 9, USDA Forest Service

Disclaimer

Contents

Conservation Assessments for Five Forest Bat Species in the Eastern United States

Frank R. Thompson, III, Editor[1]

Preface

The primary goals of this assessment are to consolidate and synthesize existing information on the status, distribution, conservation, and management considerations for five species of forest bats on national forests in Region 9: *Pipistrellus subflavus* (eastern pipistrelle), *Nycticeius humeralis* (evening bat), *Myotis austroriparius* (southeastern myotis), *M. leibii* (eastern small-footed myotis), and *M. septentrionalis* (northern long-eared bat). These species are listed as Regional Forester Sensitive Species on one or more forests of the Eastern Region. The regional forester listing affords protection for a species on the national forests for which it is listed. The forest's goal is to protect and improve the species' habitat where management practices warrant consideration of special habitat needs and to ensure that it does not become threatened or endangered.

A review of the status, biology, and management of *M. leibii* was previously completed for the George Washington and Jefferson National Forests in Region 8 (Erdle and Hobson 2001). A 1999 report produced by Bat Conservation International (Bat Conservation International 1999) summarizes information about forest bats, provides an overview of knowledge about relationships between forest bats and forest management practices, identifies practices for enhancing bat habitat, provides information on key limiting factors for Indiana bats (*M. sodalis*), presents information on the North American Bat Conservation Plan, and includes excerpts from the land management plans of many national forests. In the current assessment, authors incorporated recent information from research activities that occurred in subsequent years and summarized information on biology, natural history, and habitat necessary to address conservation issues for the five species. This assessment focuses on the national forests and States represented in the Eastern Region. It also includes information on other States within the range of each of the five species. Because of recent advances in technology and the increased focus on bat conservation, several new studies related to the five focal species have been completed or are in progress.

The assessment is organized into six chapters. The first chapter provides some general background information on forest bats and summarizes information needs for the conservation of the five species addressed in the assessment. Because of a lack of demographic information on any of these populations to assess viability, research needs and priorities are included in the background section from the perspective of theoretical constructs and approaches to obtaining the additional information needed to assess conservation and management for these species. The five subsequent chapters cover taxonomy, description, life history, habitat distribution, status, and population biology of each species.

This assessment was prepared at the request of Region 9 of the U.S. Department of Agriculture (USDA) Forest Service. The assessment highlights information needs of national forests but should also be of interest to anyone in bat conservation. Each chapter generally follows the format of other conservation assessments for species in Region 9 of the USDA Forest Service. Manuscripts were prepared by the authors, submitted to the editor, and reviewed by individuals with bat biology and conservation expertise in a blind, peer-review process overseen by the editor.

This conservation assessment consolidates and synthesizes existing information for five species of forest bats. It does not represent a management decision by the USDA Forest Service. Although authors and reviewers used the best scientific information available and consulted subject experts to prepare this document, it is expected that new information will arise. In the spirit of continuous learning and adaptive management, readers who have information that may help conserve the subject taxon, are encouraged to contact the Eastern Region of the USDA Forest Service Threatened, Endangered and Sensitive Species Program at 310 Wisconsin Avenue, Milwaukee, WI, 53203.

[1] Project leader, U.S. Department of Agriculture, Forest Service, North Central Research Station, Columbia, MO.

Acknowledgments

I thank the authors for their contributions; Fiona Reid for illustrations of the species; Bat Conservation International and Keith Geluso for distribution maps; Susan Loeb, Richard Clawson, and Tommy Parker for their review of the assessment; the North Central Research Station Communications Group for assistance with the production of the publication; and Region 9 and the Shawnee National Forest for their support of the project.

References

Bat Conservation International. 1999. Bats in eastern woodlands. Washington, DC: U.S. Department of Agriculture Forest Service; U.S. Department of the Interior, U.S. Fish & Wildlife Service; National Council for Air and Stream Improvement. 56 p. http://www.batcon.org.

Erdle, S.Y.; Hobson, C.S. 2001. Current status and conservation strategy for the eastern small-footed myotis (*Myotis leibii*). Tech. Rep. 00-19. Reston, VA: Virginia Department of Conservation and Recreation, Division of Natural Heritage. 17 p.

Status and Conservation of Five Forest Bat Species in the Eastern United States: Issues and Concerns

Sybill Amelon[1]

Bats have a higher diversity of behavior, diet, and morphology than any other mammalian order. Bats are primary predators of nocturnal insects, including many agricultural and forest pests; bats, therefore, play a key role in many forest ecosystems (Tuttle 2001). The insectivorous family Vespertilionidae (to which all five of these species belong) occurs throughout temperate and tropical areas and is the largest and most widely distributed family of bats (Koopman 1993). Despite this diversity, a relative void in knowledge exists for many of North America's bat species. This gap can be attributed in part to the fact that many of the techniques and methods used to assess habitat use or abundance for other mammals are not suitable for bats (Kunz and Kurta 1988b).

This chapter summarizes some of the conservation issues and information needs for eastern forest bats as an introduction to conservation assessments of five bat species. The concept of bat conservation initially emerged in the late 1940s and early 1950s through the efforts of several researchers (Griffin 1940, Mohr 1952). Efforts to study bats, especially those that cluster in roosts, continued through the next three decades (Fenton 1970, Kunz and Kurta 1988a, Mumford and Cope 1964, Tuttle 1976, LaVal et al. 1977). Despite these efforts, and largely due to bats' unique characteristics (small body size, volancy, nocturnal activity, low reproductive rate, and acoustic orientation), bats remain among the least studied wildlife species. Information on the ecology and population status of most North American bat species is still very limited. Technological advances in the past decade have enhanced research and conservation efforts (Kunz 2003, Kunz and Racey 1998, Barclay et al. 1996), but there continues to be a lack of methodologies and consistent, repeatable research approaches to provide the information needed to address habitat use, population status, and trends.

Twenty species of bats inhabit eastern North America at least part of the year. Of these species, four are federally listed endangered (*Myotis sodalis, M. grisescens, Corynorhinus townsendii virginianus,* and *C. t. ingens*); at least another eight species are status undetermined in part of their geographic ranges. These numbers indicate that 60 percent (at a minimum) of eastern North American bat species are experiencing population declines in part or all of their geographic ranges. (NatureServe 2002).

Declining bat populations are a concern for land management agencies throughout the Nation and also for international agencies (Kunz and Racey 1998). Conservation efforts are hampered by insufficient knowledge of factors influencing bat populations, habitat requirements, and ecosystem roles. This lack of information greatly impedes focused and comprehensive conservation management strategies. From the perspective of developing guidelines for integrating forest bat habitat needs at strategic and operational planning levels, information about the patterns of community structure and habitat use at multiple spatial and temporal scales is basic and vital (Kunz 1996). Development of effective conservation strategies for North American bat species will involve consideration of both roosting and foraging requirements, as well as the spatial distribution of these elements, during each critical life history period.

Most conservation efforts have centered on rare or endangered species. While these efforts are extremely important, more abundant species with critical ecosystem roles have been less studied. From an ecosystem perspective, conservation efforts for these species may be the most important (Pierson 1998).

Research Needed To Address Conservation Status

An ultimate goal of a conservation assessment is to address the long-term population status and viability of the species of interest. To accomplish this goal, information and data on

[1] Wildlife biologist, U.S. Department of Agriculture, Forest Service, North Central Research Station, Columbia, MO.

abundance, reproductive rate, survival rate, age structure, and mortality rate are necessary. Most of these factors are missing for each of the five forest bat species included in this conservation assessment. Therefore, a determination of whether these species are secure and likely to remain or are declining and not likely to remain, given current land management practices, can be based only on theoretical premises. Given the lack of information on these five species within Region 9 of the U.S. Department of Agriculture (USDA) Forest Service, adaptive management approaches that consider new information as it becomes available will likely be the best approaches to conserving these species.

Research and Monitoring Considerations

Methods designed to survey microchiropterans have been developed fairly recently and few researchers consider any method paramount for all species or situations (Kunz and Kurta 1988b). Traditionally, capture in mist nets or harp traps has been used to determine relative abundance of species within particular habitats (Tidemann and Woodside 1978, Tuttle 1974). Mist-netting commonly results in declines in capture rate when used on successive days (Kunz and Brock 1975, Kunz and Kurta 1988a, Stevenson and Tuttle 1982a, Humphrey et al. 1979). Bats quickly learn to avoid nets or net locations. Although capture techniques enable the collection of some demographic information (Racey 1988, Anthony et al. 1981), these techniques do not equally sample all species. In addition to unequal probability of capture, these methods usually focus on a location-specific maximum likelihood of bat activity, such as a watering site or travel corridor. The use area represented by the captures is usually unknown. Differences in foraging strategy and location (Kalko and Schnitzler 1993, Swift and Racey 1983, Walsh and Mayle 1991), temporal and spatial heterogeneity (Thomas and West 1989), observer experience (Kunz 1973), and habitat conditions (Hayes 1997, Grindal et al. 1992) may affect sampling success. Bat activity tends to vary with ambient air temperature, humidity, and insect availability; therefore, sampling sites need to be visited more than once during the sampling season to account for these temporal and environmental variations.

Temperate forest bats typically use a variety of habitats for roosting and foraging; these habitats frequently are distributed over relatively large spatial distances. Bats do not uniformly occupy all available habitats within their potential range. Habitats differ in their suitability and, therefore, in their influence on the reproductive success of animals. The diverse spatial and temporal distribution of habitats used by forest bats indicates their distribution, abundance, and conservation should be assessed at multiple spatial scales. Even with the introduction of bat detectors to allow acoustical identification of noncaptured species and miniaturized radio transmitters to improve the ability to study bat habitat use requirements, broadscale studies in North America are lacking (O'Shea and Bogen 2003).

Bats are particularly vulnerable to environmental changes affecting longevity or reproductive success (Walsh and Harris 1996). In comparison to other small mammals, bats have low reproductive rates and long life spans, characteristics that require high survival rates to ensure persistent populations (Kunz 1996). Some species have very specific roost habitat requirements; aggregations in colonies make them susceptible to elevated mortality. Loss or modification of roosting and foraging habitat may strongly affect species with these life history characteristics. It has been suggested that land-use change is one of several factors contributing to recent bat population declines (Crampton 1995, Robinson and Stebbings 1997). Reduction of large trees and snags within forested stands may affect roost availability and may increase the distance between roosting, foraging, and drinking sites. The increased energy cost of longer distances between roosting and foraging sites may be of particular importance to reproductive females (Kunz 1987). As land use changes from forested to nonforested, certain species that avoid crossing openings when commuting or foraging may be restricted from accessing distant resources (Limpens and Kapteyn 1991). Forested corridors connecting forested patches have been shown to provide valuable foraging habitat as well as travel corridors for bats between roosting and foraging sites (van Zyll de Jong 1995). No studies were found that quantified relationships between forest bat reproductive success relative to quantity and quality of roosting and foraging habitats.

Species distribution and abundance are often functions of the distribution of their resources (Brown 1984). Bats, like other animals, are closely associated with the resources of the habitats in which they live. Given the dependence of temperate bats on flying insects, considerable differences exist in their seasonal resource needs. It is impossible for insectivorous bats to remain year long in temperate climates where insects are unavailable for long periods and maintain endothermic temperature regulation; they must migrate or hibernate.

Temperate region bats are subject to selective pressures for both roosting and foraging habitats during the summer and migratory periods (Kunz 1982). When suitable habitat is available, individual species forage and optimize energy budgets in their use of habitats. While many species are flexible to some extent in their ability to use prey opportunistically within a range of habitat conditions, at some point lack of optimum habitat conditions may affect fecundity (Whitaker and Long 1998). Sympatric species may overlap in habitat or flight style, but they are probably not equally effective in catching prey compared to the energy they use (Ahlen 1981). Although their habitats may overlap, their spatial or temporal niches are sufficiently different to allow coexistence of many species in the same areas. Bats select roosts that provide suitable thermal conditions necessary for metabolic and reproductive demands (Barclay 1991, Kunz and Stern 1995), protection from predators (Fenton et al. 1983), and proximity to foraging sites (Geggie and Fenton 1985, Kunz 1982). Since most temperate region bats mate during the fall, encountering mates should not affect selection of summer habitats. Few studies have examined the relative influences of foraging and roosting requirements on bats' habitat selection.

Forests vary in structure and composition with age, productivity, and disturbance history. Therefore, the habitats they offer for bats differ in amount of foraging space and suitable roosting sites. There are conflicting indications regarding whether sympatric species of insectivorous bats' use of available habitats differs.

Existing Surveys, Monitoring, and Research

Many of the national forests in Region 9 and the associated State Departments of Natural Resources are conducting annual or biannual hibernation population counts for cave-dwelling species. In some instances, these counts are targeted at the federally listed *Myotis sodalis* (Indiana bat) and *M. grisescens* (gray bat). In other instances, hibernacula counts have the intent of counting hibernating individuals of any bat species present. In addition, many national forests are conducting summer mist-net or acoustic surveys to identify the presence and locations of forest bat species.

Survey Protocol

While mist-net surveys are fairly consistent in design and implementation, considerable variation exists in determining "on the ground" selection of mist-net locations. In addition, the overall quantity of locations recommended in the Indiana Bat Draft Recovery Plan (USFWS 1999) (a guide frequently used by national forests to design mist-net surveys) was originally designed to be used on a relatively small "project location" rather than as a tool to examine distributions over landscape-scale areas.

Research Priorities

Based on information obtained from bat researchers, U.S. Fish & Wildlife Service, recovery plans, and forest plans, the following research needs are identified with an indication of relative priority (from a species viability perspective) (Brack and Tyrell 1990; Clark 2001; Kunz 1996; Kunz and Kurta 1988b; Kunz and Robson 1995; Kurta and Murray 2002; Norberg 1998; O'Shea and Bogen 2003; Pierson 1998; Rabot 1999; Racey 1988; Stevenson and Tuttle 1982b; Taylor 2003; Turchin 1998; Tuttle 2000; USFWS 1983; Williams 2001; Barclay et al. 1996, 1999; Brigham et al. 1997; Carroll et al. 2002; Carter et al. 1999; Gopukumar et al. 2003; Webb et al. 1996).

Monitor Population Trend and Abundance

1. Develop and validate methods to assess abundance of forest bat species during nonhibernating periods. (High priority.)
2. Develop a long-term population monitoring strategy for nonhibernating periods. (High priority but subsequent to #1 above.)

Determine Terrestrial Habitat Relationships

1. Determine summer habitat use relationships (roosting and foraging) for forest bats across multiple spatial and temporal scales within the range of each species, by demographic group. This effort should be coordinated across the range of the species to provide for adequate sample size to evaluate meaningful relationships. (High priority but subsequent to Monitor Population Trend and Abundance section.)
2. Evaluate habitat quality by associating habitat parameters with reproductive success. (Due to the patchy distribution of most forest bat species, design studies using baseline or pre-treatment to post-treatment at the same location.) (High priority but subsequent #1 above and to Monitor Population Trend and Abundance section.)

References

Ahlen, I. 1981. Field identification of bats and survey methods based on sounds. Myotis. 18-19: 128-136.

Anthony, E.L.; Stack, M.H.; Kunz, T.H. 1981. Night roosting and the nocturnal time budget of the little brown bat *Myotis lucifugus*: effects of reproductive status, prey density, and environmental conditions. Oecologia. 51: 151-156.

Barclay, R.M.R. 1991. Population structure of temperate zone insectivorous bats in relation to foraging behaviour and energy demand. Journal of Animal Ecology. 60: 165-178.

Barclay, R.M.R.; Fullard, J.H.; Jacobs, D.S. 1999. Variation in the echolocation calls of the hoary bat (*laci*): influence of body size, habitat structure, and geographic location. Canadian Journal of Zoology. 77: 530-534.

Barclay, R.M.R.; Kalcounis, M.C.; Stefan, C.; et al. 1996. Can external radiotransmitters be used to assess body temperature and torpor in bats? Journal of Mammalogy. 77(4): 1102-1106.

Brack, V.; Tyrell, K. 1990. A model of the habitat used by the Indiana bat (*Myotis sodalis*) during the summer in Indiana: 1990 field studies. Indianapolis: Indiana Department of Natural Resources.

Brigham, R.M.; Grindal, S.D.; Firman, M.C.; Morissette, J.L. 1997. The influence of structural clutter on activity patterns of insectivorous bats. Canadian Journal of Zoology. 75: 131-136.

Brown, J.H. 1984. On the relationship between abundance and distribution of species. American Naturalist. 124(2): 255-279.

Carroll, S.K.; Carter, T.C.; Feldhammer, G.A. 2002. Placement of nets for bats, perception of perceived fauna. Southeastern Naturalist. 1: 193-198.

Carter, T.C.; Menzel, M.A.; Chapman, B.R.; et al. 1999. A new method to study bat activity patterns. Wildlife Society Bulletin. 27(3): 598-602.

Clark, D.R., Jr. 2001. DDT and the decline of free-tailed bats (*Tadarida brasiliensis*) at Carlsbad Caverns, New Mexico. Archives of Environmental Contamination and Toxicology. 40: 537-543.

Crampton, L. 1995. Habitat selection by bats and the potential impacts of forest fragmentation on bat populations in aspen mixed-wood forests in northern Alberta. Calgary, AB: University of Calgary. 95 p. M.S. thesis.

Fenton, M.B. 1970. Population studies of *Myotis lucifugus* in Ontario. Life Sci. Occas. Pap. Toronto, ON: Royal Ontario Museum. 77: 1-34.

Fenton, M.B.; Merriam, H.G.; Holroyd, G.L. 1983. Bats of Kootenay, Glacier and Mount Revelstoke National Parks in Canada: identification by echolocation calls, distribution and biology. Canadian Journal of Zoology. 61: 2503-2508.

Geggie, J.F.; Fenton, M.B. 1985. A comparison of foraging by *Eptesicus fuscus* (Chiroptera: Vespertilionidae) in urban and rural environments. Canadian Journal of Zoology. 63: 263-266.

Gopukumar, N.; Nathan, P.T.; Doss, P.S.; et al. 2003. Early ontogeny of foraging behaviour in the short-nosed fruit bat *Cynopterus sphinx* (Megachiroptera): preliminary results. Mammalia: Journal de Morphologie, Biologie, Systematique des Mammiferes. 67: 139-145.

Griffin, D.R. 1940. Notes on the life histories of New England cave bats. Journal of Mammalogy. 21: 181-187.

Grindal, S.D.; Collard, T.S.; Barclay, R.M.R.; Brigham, R.M. 1992. The influence of precipitation on reproduction by *Myotis* bats in British Columbia. American Midland Naturalist. 128: 339-344.

Hayes, J.P. 1997. Temporal variation in activity of bats and the design of echolocation-monitoring studies. Journal of Mammalogy. 78(2): 514-524.

Humphrey, S.R.; Baker, R.J.; Jones, J.K. 1979. Population and community ecology. In: Baker, R.J.; Jones, J.K.; Carter, D.C., eds. Biology of bats of the New World family Phyllostomatidae Part III. Spec. Pub. Mus. Texas Tech Univ. Lubbock, TX: Texas Tech University Press. 16(v3): 409-441.

Kalko, E.K.; Schnitzler, H.U. 1993. Plasticity in echolocation signals of European pipistrelle bats in search flight: implications for habitat use and prey detection. Behavioral Ecology and Sociobiology. 33: 415-428.

Koopman, K.F. 1993. Chiroptera. In: Wilson, D.E.; Reeder, D.M., eds. Mammal species of the world: a taxonomic and geographic reference. Washington, DC: Smithsonian Institution Press. http://www.nmnh.si.edu/msw/.

Kunz, T.H. 1973. Resource utilization: temporal and spatial components of bat activity in central Iowa. Journal of Mammalogy. 54: 14-32.

Kunz, T.H. 1982. Ecology of bats. New York: Plenum Press. 425 p.

Kunz, T.H. 1987. Post natal growth and energetics of suckling bats. In: Fenton, M.B.; et al., eds. Recent advances in the study of bats. Cambridge, UK: Cambridge University Press. 470 p.

Kunz, T.H. 1996. Measuring and monitoring biological diversity. In: Thomas, D.W.; et al., eds. Standard methods for mammals. Washington, DC: Smithsonian Institution Press. 409 p.

Kunz, T.H. 2003. Bat ecology. Chicago: University of Chicago Press. 779 p.

Kunz, T.H.; Brock, C.E. 1975. A comparison of mist nets and ultrasonic detectors for monitoring flight activity of bats. Journal of Mammalogy. 56: 907-911.

Kunz, T.H.; Kurta, A. 1988a. Capture methods and holding devices. In: Kunz, T.H.; Kurta, A., eds. Ecological and behavioral methods for the study of bats. Washington, DC: Smithsonian Institution Press: 1-30.

Kunz, T.H.; Kurta, A., eds. 1988b. Ecological and behavioral methods for the study of bats. Washington, DC: Smithsonian Institution Press. 533 p.

Kunz, T.H.; Racey, P.A. 1998. Bat biology and conservation. Washington, DC: Smithsonian Institution Press. 365 p.

Kunz, T.H.; Robson, S. 1995. Postnatal growth and development in the Mexican free-tailed bat (*Tadarida brasiliensis mexicana*): birth size, growth rates, and age estimation. Journal of Mammalogy. 76: 769-783.

Kunz, T.H.; Stern, A.A. 1995. Maternal investment and post-natal growth in bats. In: Racey, P.A.; Swift, S.M., eds. Ecology, evolution and behaviour of bats. Symposia of the Zoological Society of London: 123-138.

Kurta, A.; Murray, S.W. 2002. Philopatry and migration of banded Indiana bats (*Myotis sodalis*) and effects of radio transmitters. Journal of Mammalogy. 83: 585-589.

LaVal, R.K.; Clawson, R.L.; Caire, W. 1977. An evaluation of the status of myotine bats in the proposed Meramec Park Lake and Union Lake project areas, Missouri. In: Final report of myotine bat study team. Columbia, MO: University of Missouri. 136 p.

Limpens, H.G.A.; Kapteyn, K. 1991. Bats, their behavior and linear landscape elements. Myotis. 29: 39-47.

Mohr, C.E. 1952. A survey of bat banding in North America, 1932-1951. NSS Bulletin. 34: 33-47.

Mumford, R.E.; Cope, J.B. 1964. Distribution and status of the Chiroptera of Indiana. American Midland Naturalist. 72(2): 473-489.

NatureServe. 2002. NatureServe Explorer: an online encyclopedia of life [Web application]. Version 4.1. http://www.natureserve.org.

Norberg, U.M. 1998. Morphological adaptations for flight in bats. In: Kunz, T.H.; Racey, P.A., eds. Bat biology and conservation. Washington, DC: Smithsonian Institution Press: 93-108.

O'Shea, T.J.; Bogen, M. 2003. Monitoring trends in bat populations of the United States and territories: problems and prospects. Information and Technology Report USGS/BRD/ITR—2003-0003. Reston, VA: U.S. Geological Survey. 274 p.

Pierson, E.D. 1998. Tall trees, deep holes and scarred landscapes. In: Kunz, T.H.; Racey, P.A., eds. Bat biology and conservation. Washington, DC: Smithsonian Institution Press: 309-325.

Rabot, T. 1999. The Federal role in habitat protection. Endangered Species Bulletin. 24(6): 15-20.

Racey, P.A. 1988. Reproductive assessment in bats. In: Kunz, T.H., ed. Ecological and behavioral methods for the study of bats. Washington, DC: Smithsonian Institution Press: 31-46.

Robinson, M.F.; Stebbings, R.E. 1997. Home range and habitat use by the serotine bat, *Eptesicus serotinus*, in England. Journal of Zoology London. 243: 117-136.

Stevenson, D.; Tuttle, M.D. 1982a. Growth and survival of bats. In: Kunz, T.H., ed. Ecology of bats. New York: Plenum. 425 p.

Stevenson, D.E.; Tuttle, M.D. 1982b. Survivorship in the endangered gray bat, *Myotis grisescens*. Journal of Mammalogy. 62: 244-257.

Swift, S.; Racey, P.A. 1983. Resource partitioning in two species of vespertilionid bats (Chiroptera) occupying the same roost. Journal of Zoology London. 200: 249-259.

Taylor, D. 2003. Bat conservation and forest management: information needs from habitat selection studies. Bat Research News. 44: 17.

Thomas, D.W.; West, S.D. 1989. Sampling methods for bats. Gen. Tech. Report PNW-GTR-243. Portland, OR: U.S. Department of Agriculture, Forest Service, Pacific Northwest Research Station. 20 p.

Tidemann, C.R.; Woodside, D.P. 1978. A collapsible bat trap and a comparison of results obtained with the trap and mist nets. Australian Wildlife Research. 5: 355-362.

Turchin, P. 1998. Quantitative analysis of animal movement: measuring and modeling population redistribution in animals and plants. Sunderland, MA: Sinauer Associates. 405 p.

Tuttle, M.D. 1974. An improved trap for bats. Journal of Mammalogy. 55: 475-477.

Tuttle, M.D. 1976. Population ecology of the gray bat (*Myotis grisescens*): factors influencing growth and survival of newly volant young. Ecology. 57(3): 587-595.

Tuttle, M.D. 2000. Evaluation of Indiana bat hibernation requirements as they relate to recovery planning. Bat Research News. 41: 146.

Tuttle, M.D. 2001. Personal communication. Director of Bat Conservation International. Phone conversation.

U.S. Fish & Wildlife Service (USFWS). 1983. Recovery plan for the Indiana bat (revision). Washington, DC: U.S. Fish & Wildlife Service. 83 p.

USFWS. 1999. Agency draft Indiana bat (*Myotis sodalis*) revised recovery plan. Washington, DC: U.S. Fish & Wildlife Service. 53 p.

van Zyll de Jong, C.G. 1995. Habitat use and species richness of bats in a patchy landscape. Acta Theriologica. 40(3): 237-248.

Walsh, A.L.; Harris, S. 1996. Factors determining the abundance of vespertilionid bats in Britain: geographical, land class and local habitat relationships. Journal of Applied Ecology. 33: 519-529.

Walsh, A.L.; Mayle, B.A. 1991. Bat activity in different habitats in a mixed lowland woodland. Myotis. 29: 97-104.

Webb, P.I.; Speakman, J.R.; Racey, P.A. 1996. Population dynamics of a maternity colony of the pipistrelle bat (*Pipistrellus pipistrellus*) in north-east Scotland. Journal of Zoology. 240: 777-780.

Whitaker, J.O.; Long, R. 1998. Mosquito feeding by bats. Bat Research News. 39: 59-61.

Williams, M.S. 2001. Nonuniform random sampling: an alternative method of variance reduction for forest surveys. Canadian Journal of Forest Research. 31: 2080-2088.

Conservation Assessment: *Pipistrellus subflavus* (Eastern Pipistrelle) in the Eastern United States

Sybill Amelon[1]

Taxonomy and Nomenclature

The eastern pipistrelle, [*Pipistrellus subflavus* (F. Cuvier 1832) (f. L. *sub* under; *flavus* yellow—i.e., somewhat yellow)], belongs to the class Mammalia, order Chiroptera, family Vespertilionidae, subfamily Vespertilioninae, genus/species *Pipistrellus subflavus* (1959). The genus *Pipistrellus* (formerly *Vespertilio*) includes 48 species (Hornacki et al. 1982).

Four subspecies of *P. subflavus* are recognized (Davis 1959):

1. *P. s. clarus* (Baker 1954: 585). Type locality 2 miles (mi) west (W) of Jimenez, 850 feet (ft), Coahuila, Mexico.
2. *P. s. floridanus* (Davis 1957: 213). Type locality Homosassa Springs, head Homosassa River, Citrus County, Florida.
3. *P. s. subflavus* (F. Cuvier 1832: 17). Type locality Eastern United States, probably Georgia. Restricted by Davis (1959) to Le Conte Plantation, 3 mi southwest (SW) of Riceboro, Liberty County, Georgia, (*V. erthrodactylus temminck, V. monticola audubon* and *bachman,* and *obscurus miller* are synonyms).
4. *P. s. veraecruscis* (Ward 1891: 745). Type locality Las Vigas, Canton of Jalapa, Veracruz, Mexico.

P. subflavus subflavus is the most widely distributed race. Menu (1984) proposed changing the genus from *Pipistrellus* to *Perimyotis* based on dental morphology. To date, inadequate evidence exists to support this change.

Description of Species

Pipistrellus subflavus is the smallest bat found throughout the Eastern and Midwestern States. Characteristic measurements include wingspan, 200 to 260 millimeters (mm); total length, 74 to 98 mm; tail length, 30 to 46 mm; hindfoot, 7.3 to 10.5 mm; ear, 11 to 14.5 mm; forearm, 31.4 to 36 mm; and skull, 12.3 to 13.3 mm. Weight ranges from 4.6 to 7.9 grams (g). Females are consistently heavier than males. Mean female spring and fall weights are 5.8 and 7.9 g, respectively; whereas, mean male spring and fall weights are 4.6 and 7.5 g, respectively. Pelage color varies from pale yellow-orange to dark reddish-brown, to grayish-brown, and sometimes nearly black. A characteristic feature is the distinctly tricolored hair. Hairs are dark at the base and tip and lighter yellowish or brownish in the center. Juvenile pelage is darker than adult pelage. The forearm of the wing is distinctly pinkish and lighter than the dark, nearly black wing membrane. The anterior third of the uropatagium is furred. The ears are longer than they are wide and extend slightly past the end of the nose when pressed forward. The tragus is straight, tapers to a rounded tip, and is less than half the ear length. The hindfoot is large, more than half as long as the tibia. The dorsal surface of the foot and toes is covered with conspicuous hair. The calcar is not keeled; it exceeds the tibia in length. The third, fourth, and fifth metacarpals are subequal. The skull is short with a broad rostrum. The dental formula is i 2/3, c 1/1, p 2/2, m 3/3, total 34. A characteristic feature of this species is the presence of one small premolar in the upper and lower jaws (Fujita and Kunz 1984, Hamilton and Whitaker 1979).

Biology, Life History, and Natural History

Reproductive Biology and Phenology

Eastern pipistrelles are polygamous with breeding activity occurring in the fall and potentially into spring. Spermatozoa are stored in the uterus of hibernating females until spring ovulation (Guthrie 1933). Females begin arriving from hibernacula in late April (southern areas) through May (northern areas). Maximum numbers are reached from late May

[1] Wildlife biologist, U.S. Department of Agriculture, Forest Service, North Central Research Station, Columbia, MO.

to late June (south to north, respectively). Female *P. subflavus* may enter daily torpor in early weeks of pregnancy but rarely in late pregnancy and lactation (Hoying and Kunz 1998). Jones and Suttkus (1973) found male to female sex ratios were approximately equal.

The gestation period, measured from implantation to parturition, lasts at least 44 days (Wimsatt 1945). Two pups are typical, with mean litter size of 1.9 to 1.95 (Cope and Humphrey 1972, Hoying and Kunz 1998, Wimsatt 1945). The relative mass of each pup at birth (expressed as a percentage of the female's post partum body mass) ranges from 23 to 27 percent. The litter weight ranges from 44 to 54 percent (Hoying and Kunz 1998). These relative weights represent the upper extreme of maternal effort among vespertilionid bats. Parturition occurs from late May through the first 3 weeks of June in Florida (Jennings 1958); from early June to early July in Missouri (LaVal and LaVal 1980), Illinois (Feldhammer et al. 2001), Pennsylvania (Lane 1946), the city of Terre Haute in Indiana (Whitaker 1998), and eastern Massachusetts (Hoying and Kunz 1998); and from late June to early July in southern Indiana (Cope and Humphrey 1972) and Vermont (Davis 1963). These data suggest that parturition is more synchronous in northern populations.

Newborn pipistrelles are born hairless and pink with eyes closed and pinnae folded (Hoying and Kunz 1998). They are capable of making loud clicking sounds that may aid their mothers in retrieving them (Hoying and Kunz 1998). Neonates become fully furred during their first week (Whitaker 1998). Forearm length and body mass increase linearly for the first 2 weeks after birth; the rate of increase is then reduced. The relative length of the forearm reaches approximately 95 percent of adult size, and the body mass reaches 70 to 80 percent of adult mass by 3 weeks of age, the approximate time of first flight (Hoying and Kunz 1998, Whitaker 1998). Ossification of the epiphyses is nearly complete by 42 to 48 days (Hoying and Kunz 1998). Several factors may influence postnatal growth in bats; climate and food availability may be the most important (Hoying and Kunz 1998, Orr 1970, Stevenson and Tuttle 1982). Low ambient and roost temperatures may result in prolonged periods of food shortage and expenditure of energy on thermoregulation, which may contribute directly to low postnatal growth rates (Hoying and Kunz 1998). Parturition

synchrony, combined with clustering in maternity colonies, should increase metabolic rates and lead to rapid postnatal growth rates (Stevenson and Tuttle 1982, Kurta et al. 1989). If females require periods of torpor due to low temperatures and low food availability, reduced milk output and energy output to the pups could contribute to their reduced growth rate (Hoying and Kunz 1998). Whitaker (1998) described volant juveniles at approximately 4 weeks of age; these juveniles foraged with their mothers for at least an additional week. The adult females abandoned the maternity roosts soon after weaning; the juveniles remained longer.

Histological data suggest that eastern pipistrelle males behave in a manner similar to other North American vespertilionid bats in displaying testicular gametic function in summer followed by a regression of the gonads before mating and hibernation (Krutzsch and Crichton 1986). The eastern pipistrelle, however, differs in the retention of some testicular spermatozoa and the fact that only slight differences occur in summer versus winter activity of the accessory glands. These data suggest that hibernation is longer and the period of sexual quiescence is shorter in the eastern pipistrelle than in other temperate vespertilionids. Males may not reach full reproductive maturity until their second year (Krutzsch and Crichton 1986).

Subadult pipistrelles were observed to first arrive at hibernacula in early August in Missouri (LaVal and LaVal 1980). Data available from the literature suggest that differences in maturity rates vary by geographical location of the population. Davis (1963) observed that subadults in Vermont, Ontario, and Quebec had not undergone first molt and that epiphysis had not completely closed at the time of entry to hibernacula. No apparent growth occurred during hibernation, and subadults were recognized at departure from hibernacula in April and May. Conversely, subadults from West Virginia, Kentucky, and Florida molted in autumn, and the epiphyses were closed at the time of entry to hibernacula. Hoying and Kunz (1998) found epiphyses were closed by 48 days of age in Massachusetts but determined that climatic factors influenced the rate of maturity. Based on physiological conditions, estimates indicate that sexual maturity likely occurs between 3 and 15 months, depending on environmental conditions (Krutzsch and Crichton 1986, Hoying and Kunz 1998).

Ecology and Behavior

Bats require highly advanced morphological adaptations in their wing system for efficient flight (Norberg 1981, 1986; Norberg and Raynor 1987). Flight mechanics may impose significant limits on behavior; bats with different foraging behavior require differing wing structures to minimize energy costs. Norberg (1981) and Norberg and Raynor (1987) describe the wing adaptations that influence flight characteristics. Wing size is described by wing loading (WL), which is the weight (M) divided by the wing area (S) expressed in newtons per square meter (N/m^2). Slow-flying bats have large wings and low WLs; bats with smaller wings have to compensate with faster speeds for their body size. Wing shape is described by the aspect ratio (AR), which approximates narrowness of the wing. Findley et al. (1972) found the AR index to be the most useful variable in predicting flight speed.

Comparisons of wing morphology with known habitat associations suggest that bats with low ARs foraged in high-clutter forest areas, while those with high ARs foraged in areas that are more open. Forest clutter refers to the amount of interference to echolocation sound waves that exist in a particular patch of forest. The higher the density of forest vegetation, the greater the clutter effect to sound wave transmission. Farney and Fleharty (1969) examined 40 *P. subflavus* and calculated an AR of 6.92 ± 0.037 and a WL of 0.063 ± 0.002. These values indicate low WL and higher wingtip shape. Pipistrelles frequently alternate echolocation signals depending on the level of clutter encountered, indicating they are adapted to foraging in canopy gaps, edge habitats, and open habitats (Veilleux et al. 2003).

Winter hibernacula and summer maternity sites are generally in different locations (Davis 1959a; Griffin 1934, 1936; Guthrie 1933; McNab 1974a). Disproportionate sex ratios have been reported (Brack and Twente 1985, Davis 1964, Hall 1962, Jones and Pagels 1968) and attributed to higher survival rates in males and differences in selection of hibernacula between males and females. LaVal and LaVal (1980) observed large numbers of these bats captured at hibernacula in Missouri in late April and May and again in late July and August and suggested that this species may enter hibernacula earlier and leave hibernacula later than other species.

In spring, *P. subflavus* disperse from hibernacula and migrate to maternity roosts. Maternity colonies have been reported in trees, caves, and rock crevices, as well as in road culverts, buildings, and other manmade structures (Hoying and Kunz 1998, Humphrey 1975, Jones and Pagels 1968, Jones and Suttkus 1973, Lane 1946, Humphrey et al. 1976, Sandel et al. 2001, Veilleux et al. 2003). During the maternity period, sexes are segregated; females remain in small maternity colonies and males remain solitary (Findley 1954, Lane 1946). The longest migration distance recorded for *P. subflavus* was 52.8 kilometers (km). A female was banded at Sheffield, MA, in April and recovered at Katonah, NY, during hibernation. Adult female eastern pipistrelle bats at a maternity colony in eastern Massachusetts spent 77 percent of their time in day roosts at rest, 16 percent of their time alert, and 7 percent of their time grooming (Winchell and Kunz 1996). The highest activity levels occurred immediately after morning return to the roost from foraging and immediately before evening departure.

Obligate associations with other species have not been observed. Davis and Mumford (1962) observed red bats as the most consistent associate species on its feeding grounds in summer, although evening bats (*Nycticeius humeralis*), Indiana bats (*Myotis sodalis*), big brown bats (*Eptesicus fuscus*), and silver-haired bats (*Lasionycteris noctivagans*) were also collected in shotgun samplings.

Echolocation characteristics in open habitats indicate the eastern pipistrelle produces 5 milliseconds (ms) of frequency modulated/constant frequency (FM/CF) echolocation calls. Two harmonics have been noted: the first with energy between 35 and 19 kilohertz (kHz) and the second with energy between 70 and 38 kHz (MacDonald et al. 1994).

Hibernation

Mammalian hibernation is characterized by periods of torpor interrupted cyclically by spontaneous arousal. Individuals aroused during hibernation tend to fly or move around between periods of torpor. Eastern pipistrelles appear to be obligate hibernators (Brack and Twente 1985, McNab 1974a, Sandel et al. 2001). Hibernation occurs singly or in very small groups in caves, mines, road culverts, and other manmade structures and is often associated with other species including *Myotis lucifugus, M. grisescens, M. septentrionalis, M. austroriparius,*

M. sodalis, and *Eptesicus fuscus* (Brack and Twente 1985, Davis 1964, McNab 1974b, Mumford and Whitaker 1975, Myers 1964, Sandel et al. 2001). Eastern pipistrelles frequently use portions of hibernacula with constant, lower temperatures (Fitch 1966, Hall 1962) and higher humidity (Ploskey and Sealer 1979).

The expenditure rate of energy during hibernation is a critical factor affecting survival of the eastern pipistrelle bat. Ploskey and Sealer (1979) estimated the minimum quantity of fat required by eastern pipistrelles at the beginning of hibernation to be 0.91 g fat/g fat-free dry mass. An average-weight eastern pipistrelle bat (4.6 to 5.6 g) entering hibernation would need to weigh 6 to 8 g. Fat-free dry mass remains relatively constant throughout the hibernation period. Fat content varies seasonally, with the highest fat index occurring in October and the lowest in May (Ploskey and Sealer 1979). Females had significantly larger fat deposits, which may be a source of extra energy needed for gestation or may simply reflect differences in metabolism or hormonal balance between the sexes (Herreid 1964). During hibernation, male *P. subflavus* decrease in mass from September to April, while females decrease in mass from September to March (Fitch 1966). Total loss of mass for males is higher (39 percent) than for females (29 percent).

In laboratory experiments with *P. subflavus* found hibernating, individuals responded to increasing temperatures by increasing heart rate (Davis and Reite 1967). When temperatures approached 0 °C, bats aroused from hibernation. McNab (1974a) found *P. subflavus* to be an obligate hibernator even in Florida, where ambient temperatures remain high even in cave environments. The inability to avoid hibernation was attributed to the species' reproductive requirements; in particular, the long period of torpor required for successful sperm storage in the female. Krutzsch and Crichton (1986) suggested that the reproductive period is extended in this species as a function of increased duration of hibernation, that testicular spermatozoa persist longer, and that accessory glands are not differentiated between winter and spring/summer. Pipistrelles, more frequently than other temperate hibernating bats, remain in deep torpor for longer periods between arousals from hibernation. Some have suggested that this length of torpor may be related to the pipistrelle's smaller size and longer total time spent in hibernation (McNab 1974a). Brack and Twente (1985) found a period

of 111 days was the maximum duration of hibernation between arousals for eastern pipistrelle bats.

The eastern pipistrelle bat is capable of a 30-fold range in aerobic metabolism between hypothermia of hibernation and foraging flight (Lechner 1985). Examination of bats between fall (mean body weight = 6.22 g) and spring (mean body weight = 4.58 g) revealed no significant differences for total lung volume, alveolar surface area, mean septal thickness, or membrane diffusing capacity. Lechner (1985) found, despite the loss of 13 percent of fresh weight for both the heart and lungs and 25 percent for the liver during hibernation, blood-free protein and DNA content were not altered, indicating resistance to hibernation-induced proteolysis.

Food Habits

Analysis of stomach contents (Whitaker 1972) and analysis of fecal pellets (Brack and Finni 1987, Griffith and Gates 1985) revealed that the diet of *P. subflavus* consists of species of coleopterans, homopterans, dipterans, hymenopterans, and lepidopterans. Prey items primarily consist of small insects ranging in size from 4 to 10 mm in length. Lepidopterans were found to be consumed more than relative availability and coleopterans and homopterans less than relative availability in Georgia (Carter et al. 1998). Carter et al. (2003) examined fecal pellets from 27 eastern pipistrelle bats in West Virginia and found their diet to be highly variable. Lepidoptera, coleoptera, hymenoptera, hemiptera, diptera, homoptera, and tricoptera were fairly equally represented.

Mortality and Predation Factors

Based on fall hibernacula counts of subadults and juveniles, juvenile mortality during the period of early flight may be as high as 50 percent (Hoying and Kunz 1998). Failure to store sufficient fat reserves may cause significant mortality among subadults during the first hibernation period (Davis 1966). Mortality from predation, accidents, disturbance, and inclement weather has been documented although no consistent predators or causes of mortality were noted (Gillette and Kimbrough 1970). Predators included a vole (Martin 1961), a frog (Creel 1963), an American swallow-tailed kite (Lee and Clark 1993), and a hoary bat (*Lasiurus cinereus*) (Bishop 1947). Mortality from flooding (Baker 1978) and snowstorms (Rysgaard 1941) have been recorded.

Mortality from bands has been reported in several bat species. Improved band designs have become available within recent years, although even these improved designs may not be appropriate for all species. Nationally coordinated banding efforts still do not exist in North America.

Endoparasites include trematodes; when infected, helminth load is highest in autumn (Nickel and Hansen 1967). Ectoparasites include chiggers, with reported infestation rates of 23 to 24 percent, and spinturnicid mites (Whitaker and Loomis 1979, Whitaker and Mumford 1973).

Longevity

The highest longevity record for *P. subflavus* is for a male that was captured in Illinois 14.8 years after its initial capture (Walley and Jarvis 1971). Other records include ages of approximately 11 years (Paradiso and Greenhall 1966), 10 years (Mohr 1952), and 6 years (Hitchcock 1965). Davis and Hitchcock (1965) reported high mortality of juveniles during their second summer. Davis (1966) stated that high mortality occurs between the first and second hibernation periods, most likely during winter. Jones and Pagels (1968) argued that, because survivorship was based on band return at a specific location, variation in survivorship observed by Davis (1966) could not be distinguished from the dispersal of individuals to new areas.

Banding Data

Banding efforts by Miller and Allen (1928) marked initial attempts to study migration in North American bats. Four *P. subflavus* bats were banded and subsequently recovered 3 years later when they returned to the summer roost where they were initially banded. Success of banding studies is highly variable, largely based on the species of study and the questions being addressed. Some species are less likely to be recaptured at summering sites due to trap avoidance, and some species are more sensitive to banding injuries. Due largely to these limitations, large-scale banding efforts were abandoned (Greenhall and Paradiso 1968).

Site Fidelity

High site fidelity (30 to 60 percent) has been reported for *P. subflavus* for hibernacula (Hahn 1908, Menzel et al. 1999),

with many individuals remaining in the same location within hibernacula for several weeks (Veilleux et al. 2003).

Fewer studies have examined site fidelity associated with maternity colonies. Whitaker (1998) observed six maternity colonies in buildings in Indiana and found *P. subflavus* to switch roosts frequently during the maternity period both with and without volant young. These observations suggest that even in this species, which has a high litter mass to maternal weight ratio, the practice of roost switching (and moving young) is a common occurrence similar to that documented for this and other tree-roosting species. Jones and Suttkus (1973), working in Louisiana, found nearly 60 percent of the females observed used only one building as a roosting site. Females were observed to have higher site fidelity to roosting location than males did. Males observed roosting in the same study area were found to have lower site fidelity to a single building. Veilleux et al. (2001) examined roost site fidelity for 18 pregnant or lactating females and found these bats used 2.8 ± 1.7 roost trees and changed trees 2.3 ± 1.9 times, on average. Colony sizes were found to be similar before and after roost changes, suggesting that colonies may change roosts as groups.

Distribution

P. subflavus occurs throughout most of eastern North and Central America and into parts of the Midwestern United States (Fujita and Kunz 1984). The eastern border of the range of the subspecies *subflavus* follows the Atlantic coast from Georgia to Nova Scotia. Broders et al. (2001) reported new records from southern coastal New Brunswick. The northern border extends from central Minnesota eastward through southeastern Ontario and Quebec. Minimal records are reported from southeastern Michigan (Kurta 1982). The southwestern border extends from the Edwards Plateau in Texas south to Tamaulipas, Mexico (Davis 1959b). The Gulf of Mexico along Florida's panhandle marks the southern border of the range. *P. s. floridanus* occurs throughout peninsular Florida and southeastern Georgia. *P. s. clarus* extends from northern Coahuila, Mexico, to Texas and is separated from the range of *P. s. subflavus* by the Rio Grande Valley (Davis 1959a). *P. s. veraecrucis* is known from tropical lowlands and mountainous sections of eastern Mexico and northeastern Honduras (Davis 1959a). Brack and Mumford (1984) indicated accordance between the southern limit of the Wisconsinan glaciation and the northern range of the pipistrelle; they pointed out that captures north of the glacial limit were always along riparian habitats. Barbour and Davis (1969) stated that the bat was found over watercourses but not over forests or fields. Recently, western range expansion has been documented (Geluso et al. 2004) (fig. 1).

Figure 1. *Westward range expansion of the eastern pipistrelle (*Pipistrellus subflavus*) in the United States, including new records (open circles) from New Mexico, South Dakota, and Texas.*

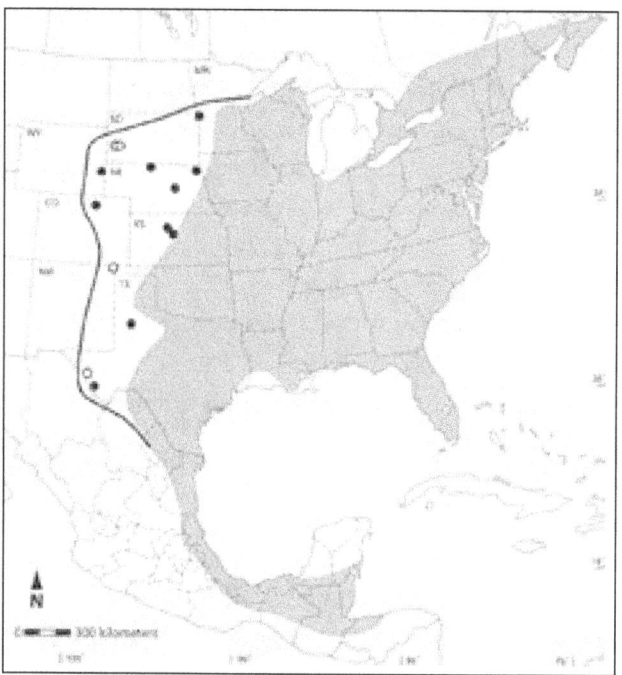

Source: Geluso et al. 2004.

Habitat Requirements

Maternity Period (May to August)

Roosting Habitat

Veilleux et al. (2003) found lactating female pipistrelle bats in Indiana roosting exclusively in dead clusters of leaves (65 percent), live foliage (30 percent), or squirrels nests (5 percent). Frequently used tree species include several oaks. Mean roost tree height was 20.8 m ± 7.1 stand density (SD). Roost height from the ground was 15.7 ± 6.8 m. Roost tree diameter at breast height was 33.2 centimeters ± 18.8 SD.

Bats remained at roost trees for 6 days, on average, before moving to new roosts; they traveled approximately 19 to 139 m between roost trees. *P. subflavus* have been noted to roost among the foliage of trees (Davis and Mumford 1962, Findley 1954, Veilleux et al. 2003), in buildings (Whitaker 1998), in the twilight zone of caves (Humphrey and Cope 1976), and in Spanish moss (Davis and Mumford 1962). Menzel et al. (1999) reported an individual female roosting in live oak trees in the understory of an oak-pine community type. Other tree species used by this individual included *Ilex vomitoria, Vaccinnium arboreum, Persea borbonia,* and *Pinus spp.* This female also roosted in clumps of Spanish moss. Lacki and Hutchinson (1999) observed eastern pipistrelles roosting in rock shelters and cliffs in Kentucky. The general landscapes used by eastern pipistrelles include partly open country with large trees and woodland edges.

Foraging Habitat

P. subflavus seem to prefer watercourses for foraging but are not restricted to these sites (Davis and Mumford 1962). *P. subflavus* primarily feed over water and at forest edges (Barley 1923, Blair 1935, Bowles 1975, Schmidly et al. 1977). This species uses farm ponds and other water sources provided some trees are available in the vicinity (Barbour and Davis 1969, Davis and Mumford 1962). This species has a relatively slow, erratic pattern of flight (Hoying and Kunz 1998, Paradiso 1969). Gould (1955) reported pipistrelles to have acquired 1.4 to 1.7 g of food during a 30-minute foraging bout. Foraging behavior of light-tagged eastern pipistrelles included long sessions of foraging activity (84 to 294 seconds per foraging episode) just over the top of streamside vegetation and taller streamside trees (Harvey 1999, Caire et al. 1984). This species is believed to intermittently forage from dusk to midnight and then have another period of feeding activity toward dawn. Veilleux et al. (2003) found eastern pipistrelle females foraging up to 4.3 km from their roost locations.

Hibernation Period (October to April)

P. subflavus use caves, mines, and rock crevices as hibernation sites in winter, roosting in warmer parts of the cave or mine (Speakman et al. 1991). This species is believed to rarely fly outside the hibernation site in winter (Whitaker and Rissler

1992) and to accept full gates on the caves or mines used for hibernation (Currie 1999). Menzel et al. (1999) found the average humidity of female *P. subflavus* roosting sites to be higher than those used by males (64.2 percent and 61.5 percent, respectively) during hibernation in Georgia mines. Roost height and temperature were not different between sexes; temperatures of −6 to14 °C have been documented (Barbour and Davis 1969, McNab 1974b, Sandel et al. 2001). This temperature range is among the highest documented for eastern forest bat species (Rabinowitz 1981). Other factors found to positively correlate with higher roosting densities are presence of standing water, size of mine entrance, and gradient of mine entrance (Menzel et al. 1999). Minimum temperature was found to be a significant predictor of pipistrelle abundance at hibernating locations in Texas, with occupancy being greatest in December and January (Sandel et al. 2001). In Arkansas, eastern pipistrelle bats used 54 of 93 surveyed caves (Briggler and Prather 2003). The bats tended to use larger caves with higher thermal stability and east-facing openings. More eastern pipistrelle bats were found in caves with a wider range of temperature regimes within a season but less variation between seasons.

Potential Threats

Natural or Human Factors
Factors contributing to bat population declines have been attributed to pesticide poisoning (Geluso 1976, Reidinger 1976, Tuttle 1979), chemical pollution, siltation of waterways (Hall 1962, Tuttle 1979), flooding (Hall 1962), and disturbance by humans (Clark and Alexander 1983, Clark and Lamont 1976, Clark and Rattner 1987, Currie 1999, Fenton 1970, Humphrey 1978, O'Shea and Clark 2001, Reidinger and Cockrum 1978, Sheffield and Chapman 1992, Tuttle 1981, Esher et al. 1980, Humphrey et al. 1976). Disturbance during the hibernation or maternity periods is a significant factor in the widespread decline of cave- and mine-dependent bat species (Clark and Alexander 1983, Clark et al. 1983). The foremost factor leading to population declines is unwarranted destruction of roost sites, particularly hibernacula (Cope et al. 1991). North American bat conservation efforts have therefore focused primarily on protecting hibernacula from vandalism and physical alterations.

Food chain poisoning by pesticides—in particular insecticides such as organochlorines and anticholinesterase—has been demonstrated to have negative impacts on insectivorous bats (Powell 1983). Lipids of brown fat from four species of hibernating bats in Maryland (including *P. subflavus*) contained significantly higher concentrations of DDE (FIA 2003) than those found in white fat. Brown fat facilitates arousal from hibernation by producing heat through rapid metabolism of triglycerides. In vitro, *P. subflavus* brain ATPases were sensitive to DDT and DDE at concentrations considerably below environmental levels (Esher et al. 1980). A single *P. subflavus* collected along Virginia's Holston River contained elevated levels of mercury (Hg), suggesting a possible relationship to Hg-contaminated industrial effluents.

Present or Potential Risks to Habitat
Although there is still much to learn about this species' maternity and winter habitat requirements, initial information concerning summer habitat indicates use of deciduous forest trees in landscapes that include interspersed nonforested patches. Since this habitat is widespread and abundant in Eastern North America, the primary risk to habitat may involve availability and suitability of winter habitat or pesticide exposure in summer habitats. The widespread recreational use of caves and indirect or direct disturbance by humans during the hibernation period pose the greatest known threat to this species. Because of this species' consistent use of deep torpor during hibernation, response to nontactile disturbance in the form of lights and movement near hibernating locations may not be detectable until well after the activities occur. Bats in deep torpor may take an hour or more to arouse from disturbance. In addition, this species hibernates singly, often in very accessible locations within hibernacula, which, in combination with slow arousal, makes *P. subflavus* highly susceptible to tactile disturbance or persecution.

Inadequacy of Existing Regulatory Mechanisms
Early bat roost protection efforts focused on eliminating or reducing disturbances by installing informative signs or "bat friendly" gates and fences. The purpose was to control human disturbance during critical hibernation and maternity periods. In some cases, these efforts were disadvantageous because of

limited understanding of bat behavior and cave microclimate factors. Early gate designs in some instances restricted natural air flow patterns, resulting in inappropriate temperatures during at least some portion of the hibernation period.

Protecting natural and manmade winter roosting structures would be one of the highest priorities for this species. Funding to facilitate these protection measures is often unavailable for nonlisted species.

Population Status

Rangewide
Both Global Heritage Status and National Heritage Status are "5," indicating the species is globally and nationally demonstrably widespread and common.

State
Individual State Heritage Status is described in State Summaries and in table 1.

Table 1. *Population status of* Pipistrellus subflavus *by State[1].*

State or province	Status[2]	Current estimate	Summer habitat (reported)	Winter habitat (reported)
Alabama	S5			Caves
Arkansas	S4			Caves
Connecticut	S4			
Delaware	S5			
Florida	SU			
Georgia	S5	Common in the mountains and piedmont; locally abundant on the coastal plain	At forest edges, over forest canopy, and over bodies of water	Caves, rock crevices, old mines, hollow trees, buildings, and clumps of Spanish moss
Illinois	S5			Caves
Indiana	S4		Buildings and trees	Caves
Iowa	S4			
Kansas	S4		Rocky areas, buildings, and trees	Caves, mines, and sinkholes
Kentucky	S4, S5	Common across Kentucky in summer and during migration; nearly every cave across the State harbors at least a few hibernating individuals	Hollow trees and buildings; in forest understory, along stream corridors, and along woodland edges	Caves, mines quarries, and sinkholes
Louisiana	S4, S5			
Maine	SU			
Massachusetts	S4			
Michigan	S2			
Minnesota	S3			
Mississippi	S5			
Missouri	SU		Buildings, trees, and rock crevices	Caves and mines

Table 1. *Population status of* Pipistrellus subflavus *by State[1] (continued).*

State or province	Status[2]	Current estimate	Summer habitat (reported)	Winter habitat (reported)
Nebraska	S1			
New Hampshire	S1			
New Jersey	SU			
New York	S3			
North Carolina	S5			
Ohio	S?			
Oklahoma	S4		Forests and woodlands	Caves, buildings, and rocky crevices
Pennsylvania	S4, S5		Trees	Caves, buildings, and rocky crevices
Rhode Island	S4			
South Carolina	S?			
Tennessee	S5			
Texas	S5		Forested streams	Box culverts
Vermont	S3			
Virginia	S5			
West Virginia	S5			Caves and mines
Wisconsin	S3, S4			
New Brunswick	S2			
Nova Scotia	S1			
Ontario	S3			

[1] Information about population and habitat use is based on literature cited. See text and References section.

[2] Status based on Natural Heritage State Rarity ranks (NatureServe 2002). S1: Extremely rare; usually 5 or fewer occurrences in the State, or, in the case of communities, covering less than 50 hectares (ha) in aggregate; or may have a few remaining individuals; often especially vulnerable to extirpation. S2: Very rare; usually between 5 and 20 occurrences, or, in the case of communities, covering less than 250 ha in aggregate; or few occurrences with many individuals; often susceptible to becoming endangered. S3: Rare to uncommon; usually between 20 and 100 occurrences; may have fewer occurrences, but with a large number of individuals in some populations; may be susceptible to large-scale disturbances. S4: Common; usually more than 100 occurrences, but may be fewer with many large populations; may be restricted to only a portion of the State; usually not susceptible to immediate threats. S5: Very common; secure under present conditions. SU: Status uncertain, often because of low search efforts or cryptic nature of the element.

Habitat Status

Summary of Land Ownership and Existing Habitat Protection

National Forests

Estimates of the potential available habitat for *P. subflavus* were based on U.S. Department of Agriculture (USDA) Forest Service Forest Inventory and Analysis (FIA) data, which estimate the amount of upland hardwood and pine-hardwood forest land more than 60 years old for all States with national forests in Regions 8 and 9 (Southern and Eastern Forest Service Regions combined to look at the entire species range) and Region 9 (examined alone to look at potential available habitat for States in the Eastern Region), excluding rarely used deciduous forest types (such as aspen). This coarse-scale assessment of habitat availability considers forest type and age class based on USDA Forest Service FIA data (FIA 2003); this analysis does not consider other aspects of forest structure that may influence use by this species. The database used is subject to sampling errors associated with coarse-scale inventory. Estimates were for the acreage of upland hardwood and pine-hardwood forest land for forests of all ownerships, including other federally owned, State-owned, county/municipal-owned, and privately owned lands within these States. Approximately 5.9 percent of upland hardwood, bottom-land hardwood, and pine-hardwood forest types occur on National Forest System (NFS) lands within the eastern range of this species; 2.9 percent occur on NFS lands within Region 9 (figs. 2 and 5). Estimates indicated that 358,219,772 potential acres of upland hardwood, bottom-land hardwood, and pine-hardwood forest land that could potentially serve as foraging habitat occur within the eastern range of this species. Estimates also indicate that stands more than 60 years old in upland hardwood and pine-hardwood forest types would provide suitable trees to meet the roosting requirements of this species. Within the eastern range of this species, estimates indicate that 330,457,331 acres occur and 88,687,204 acres, or 27 percent, of the total available are more than 60 years old (figs. 3 and 4). On NFS lands within Region 9, estimates indicate 9,671,251 acres of potential

Figure 2. *Ownership of upland hardwood, bottom-land hardwood, and pine-hardwood forest types within the eastern range of* P. subflavus.

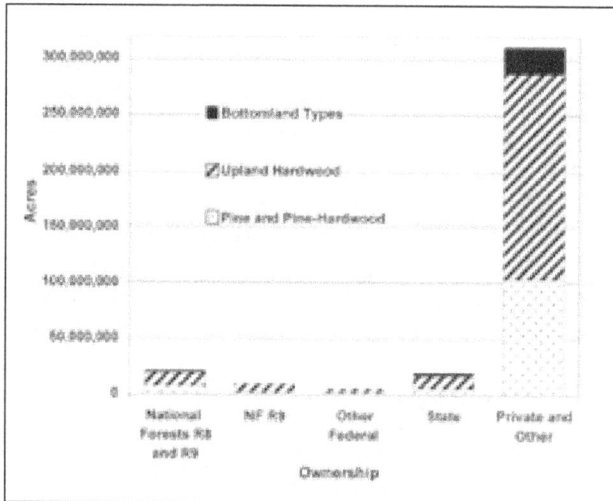

Alabama, Arkansas, Connecticut, Delaware, Florida, Georgia, Illinois, Indiana, Iowa, Kansas, Kentucky, Louisiana, Maine, Massachusetts, Michigan, Minnesota, Mississippi, Missouri, Nebraska, New Hampshire, New Jersey, New York, North Carolina, Ohio, Oklahoma, Pennsylvania, Rhode Island, South Carolina, Tennessee, Texas, Vermont, Virginia, West Virginia, Wisconsin.

Figure 3. *Acreage by ownership of upland hardwood forest type and percentage of upland hardwood forest type more than 60 years old by ownership within the eastern range of* P. subflavus.

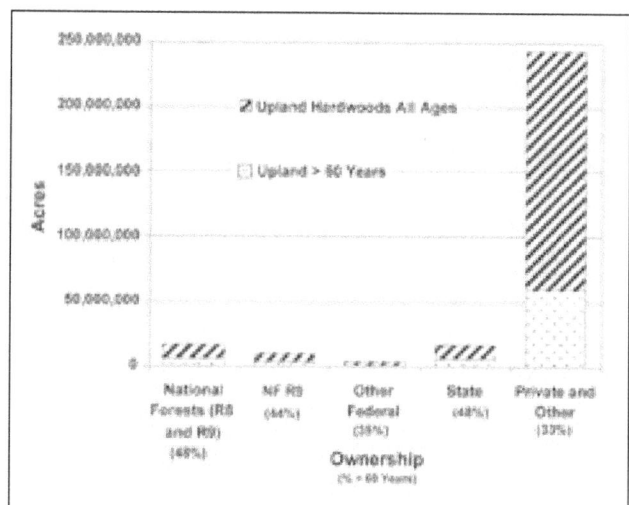

Alabama, Arkansas, Connecticut, Delaware, Florida, Georgia, Illinois, Indiana, Iowa, Kansas, Kentucky, Louisiana, Maine, Massachusetts, Michigan, Minnesota, Mississippi, Missouri, Nebraska, New Hampshire, New Jersey, New York, North Carolina, Ohio, Oklahoma, Pennsylvania, Rhode Island, South Carolina, Tennessee, Texas, Vermont, Virginia, West Virginia, Wisconsin.

Conservation Assessments for Five Forest Bat Species in the Eastern United States

Figure 4. *Acreage by ownership of pine and pine-hardwood forest types and percentage of pine and pine-hardwood forest types more than 60 years old by ownership within the eastern range of* P. subflavus.

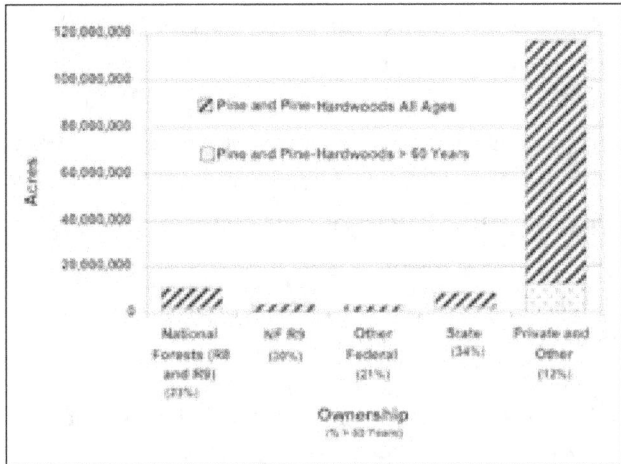

Alabama, Arkansas, Connecticut, Delaware, Florida, Georgia, Illinois, Indiana, Iowa, Kansas, Kentucky, Louisiana, Maine, Massachusetts, Michigan, Minnesota, Mississippi, Missouri, Nebraska, New Hampshire, New Jersey, New York, North Carolina, Ohio, Oklahoma, Pennsylvania, Rhode Island, South Carolina, Tennessee, Texas, Vermont, Virginia, West Virginia, Wisconsin.

Figure 5. *Acreage by ownership of bottom-land hardwood forest type and percentage of bottom-land hardwood forest type more than 60 years old by ownership within the eastern range of* P. subflavus.

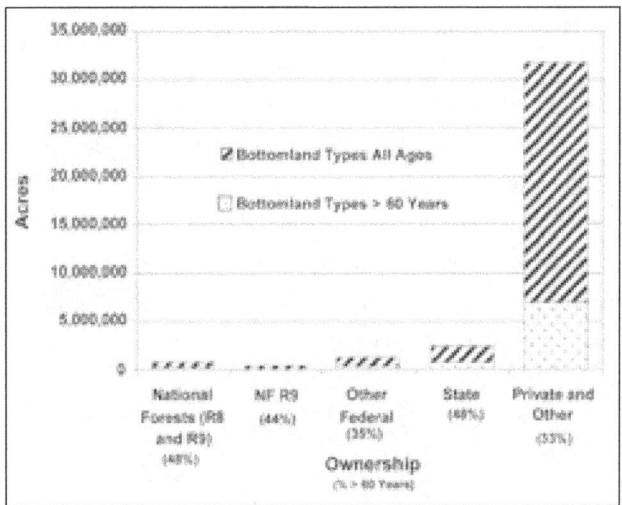

Alabama, Arkansas, Connecticut, Delaware, Florida, Georgia, Illinois, Indiana, Iowa, Kansas, Kentucky, Louisiana, Maine, Massachusetts, Michigan, Minnesota, Mississippi, Missouri, Nebraska, New Hampshire, New Jersey, New York, North Carolina, Ohio, Oklahoma, Pennsylvania, Rhode Island, South Carolina, Tennessee, Texas, Vermont, Virginia, West Virginia, Wisconsin.

foraging habitat (upland hardwood, bottom-land hardwood, and pine-hardwood forest types) and 3,786,768 acres of upland hardwood and pine-hardwood forest types more than 60 years old (40.3 percent) are available for roosting (figs. 3 and 4).

State Summaries

Illinois. State status is very common (S5, table 1). Mist-net surveys at 41 sites within the Shawnee National Forest during the summers of 1999 and 2000 resulted in the capture of 417 bats of 10 species. Eastern pipistrelles were caught most frequently in edge habitats.

Indiana. State status is common (S4, table 1). Mumford and Cope (1964) noted *P. subflavus* as a common, permanent resident more commonly found in summer than winter. Winter activity of bats at Copperhead Cave, an abandoned clay mine, was monitored in 1989. Although eastern pipistrelles were noted in hibernation, only 13 were found to be active during midwinter (Johnson 2001). Surveys at 27 abandoned coal mine entrances between 1984 and 1996 found eastern pipistrelles

using 11 of the sites (Kurta 2000). A colony of pipistrelles originally located in 1959 in a building was no longer present in 1989 (Kurta 2001). During late summer and fall (August through October), *P. subflavus* was the most frequently captured bat in abandoned Indiana coal mines (1.7 per visit) (Whitaker and Stacy 1996).

Michigan. State status is very rare; usually between 5 and 20 occurrences (S2, table 1). *P. subflavus* will likely be listed as a "species at risk" for the Ottawa National Forest's upcoming forest plan (Unger and Kurta 1998). Records show pipistrelles are associated with abandoned early 20th century copper, iron, and silver mines scattered across the forest (Johnson 2001). Broders et al. (2001) pointed out that the species' range extends into glaciated New Brunswick and Nova Scotia, likely because of the presence of suitable hibernacula.

No pipistrelles were caught with extensive mist-net procedures in the Huron-Manistee National Forests during the summer of 1998 and 1999 (Tibbels and Kurta 2003). Only two captures of pipistrelles were reported from swarming surveys in the Huron-Manistee National Forests at a dam during 12 nights between August 23 and September 24, 1998 and 1999 (Knowles 1992). One bat was tracked to a healthy white oak (*Quercus alba*) in the middle of a shelterwood cut and later to a healthy red oak (*Q. rubra*), where it apparently roosted in leaves near the top (about 20 m high). A second pipistrelle roosted in the foliage of a white oak. Other sources also indicate that pipistrelles may roost in clusters of dead leaves (Williamson 2001).

In a study of bat use of red pine (*Pinus resinosa*) forests in the Huron-Manistee National Forests, acoustic methods identified pipistrelles in unthinned open stands and thinned stands but not in normal unthinned red pine stands (Trombulak et al. 2001).

Broders et al. (2001) believed that the distribution of pipistrelles in Canada was influenced by the availability of hibernacula, primarily "solution caves" formed by water dissolving holes in limestone or similar rocks. Pipistrelles in New Brunswick, Canada, foraged over water (Broders et al. 2001).

As safety work is completed on abandoned mine shafts on the Ottawa National Forest, provisions will be made to keep mines "bat friendly" while keeping people out (Johnson 2001).

Minnesota. State status is rare to uncommon (S3, table 1). Although an occurrence is recorded in northern Minnesota (Lacki and Bookhout 1983), *P. subflavus* occurs primarily in the southern half of the State. The species is located considerably east of the Chippewa National Forest (Dunn and Hall 1989), where no occurrences of this species are known. Although the range was previously thought not to include northern Minnesota, two individual hibernators have been collected in northeast Minnesota (Williamson 2001).

Missouri. State status is undetermined (SU, table 1). Extensive surveys for forest bats have been conducted on the Mark Twain National Forest from 1997 to present (Amelon 2001). Trapping sites have included upland ponds and trails, streams and rivers, roads, caves, and mines. A geographical area or habitat appears to be associated with this species' distribution pattern. In 1999, only nine eastern pipistrelles were captured during summer surveys in riparian and upland habitats within the south central portion of the State. All individuals captured were males.

During 2001 and 2003 surveys that also took place in riparian and upland habitats within central and southeast portions of the State, only 10 to 12 percent of total captures were eastern pipistrelles. During 2002 surveys in the southwest portion of the State, nearly 20 percent of captures were eastern pipistrelles (20 percent females, 80 percent males). In the areas with a higher percentage of eastern pipistrelles represented, females were most frequently captured along streams and males were fairly evenly distributed between riparian and upland habitats. Eastern pipistrelles were well represented in fall hibernacula surveys.

New Hampshire. State status is extremely rare; usually five or fewer occurrences (S1, table1).

Ohio. State status is undetermined (S?, table 1). Distribution and activity of bats on the Wayne National Forest were studied in the summer and winter of 1979 and 1980. Surveys were conducted at abandoned mines and riparian sites. *P. subflavus* represented 13 percent of the summer captures and was found to use some of the mines for hibernation (Sanders 2000).

Pennsylvania. State status is common to very common (S4, S5; table 1). Between 1980 and 1988, 190 abandoned mines and caves were surveyed for hibernating bats. Hibernating bats were found at 71 percent of the surveyed sites; eastern pipistrelle bats were found at 56 percent of the sites, representing the widest distribution of the species found hibernating (Dunn and Hall 1989).

Vermont. State status is rare to uncommon (S3, table 1). Trapping records from Dorset Cave and Greely Talc Mine indicate low numbers of eastern pipistrelles (two) were captured among 4,065 bats captured in September 2000. Surveys conducted at Dorset Cave between 1935 and 2001 indicate that total numbers of bats observed show no obvious trend over time. Cave surveys in Vermont indicate *P. subflavus* has been present in low numbers throughout the entire period (Geluso et al. 2004).

Dorset Cave was gated in 1985 but may need modifications to improve conditions. This site is an important bat resource in Vermont. Sanders (2000) recommended that this site be closed to recreation year round. Forest bat surveys conducted in 1999 found that 126 bats representing five species were found to be using areas in or near the Green Mountain National Forest; *P. subflavus* was not found in this survey (Amelon 2001).

West Virginia. State status is very common (S5, table 1).

Wisconsin. State status is rare to common (S3, S4; table 1). This bat is not documented on the Chequamegon-Nicolet National Forest, but the Wisconsin Natural Resources Natural Heritage database indicates that it is documented in Crawford, Grant, Iowa, Lafayette, Pierce, Richland, and Vernon Counties.

References

Amelon, S.K. 2001. Unpublished data. Columbia, MO: U.S. Department of Agriculture, Forest Service, North Central Research Station.

Baker, R.R. 1978. The evolutionary ecology of animal migration. New York: Holmes and Meier. 1012 p.

Barbour, R.W.; Davis, W.H. 1969. Bats of America. Lexington, KY: University of Kentucky Press. 286 p.

Barley, V. 1923. Mammals of the District of Columbia. In: Proceedings, Biological Society of Washington. Washington, DC. 36: 103-138.

Bishop, S.C. 1947. Curious behavior of a hoary bat. Journal of Mammalogy. 28: 293-294.

Blair, W.F. 1935. The mammals of a Florida hammock. Journal of Mammalogy. 16: 271-277.

Bowles, J.B. 1975. Distribution and biogeography of mammals of Iowa. Spec. Pub. Mus. 9: 1-184.

Brack, V.J.; Finni, G.R. 1987. Mammals of southern Clermont County, Ohio, with notes on the food habits of four species of bats. Ohio Journal of Science. 87(4): 130-133.

Brack, V.J.; Mumford, R.E. 1984. The distribution of *Pipistrellus subflavus* and the limit of the Wisconsinan glaciation: an interface. American Midland Naturalist. 112(2): 397-401.

Brack, V.J.; Twente, J.W. 1985. The duration of the period of hibernation of three species of vespertilionid bats. Canadian Journal of Zoology. 63: 2952-2954.

Briggler, J.T.; Prather, J.W. 2003. Seasonal use and selection of caves by the eastern pipistrelle bat (*Pipistrellus subflavus*). American Midland Naturalist. 149: 406-412.

Broders, H.G.; McAlpine, D.F.; Forbes, G.J. 2001. Status of the eastern pipistrelle (*Pipistrellus subflavus*) in New Brunswick. Northeastern Naturalist. 8(3): 331-336.

Caire, W.; Smith, J.F.; Royce, M.A.; McGuire, S. 1984. Early foraging behavior of insectivorous bats in western Oklahoma. Journal of Mammalogy. 65(2): 319-324.

Carter, T.C.; Menzel, M.A.; Edwards, J.W.; Sheldon, O.F.; Menzel, J.M.; Ford, W.M. 2003. Food habits of seven species of bats in the Allegheny Plateau and Ridge and Valley of West Virginia. Northeast Naturalist. 10: 83-88.

Carter, T.C.; Menzel, M.A.; Warnell, D.B.; Krishon, D.M.; Laerm, J. 1998. Prey selection by five species of vespertilionid bats on Sapelo Island, Georgia. Brimleyana. 25: 158-170.

Clark, D.R.; Bunck, C.M.; Cromartie, E.; LaVal, R.K. 1983. Year and age effects on residues of dieldrin and heptachlor in dead gray bats, Franklin County, Missouri—1976, 1977, and 1978. Environmental Toxicology and Chemistry. 2: 387-393.

Clark, D.R.; Rattner, B.A. 1987. Orthene toxicity to little brown bats (*Myotis lucifugus*): acetylcholinesterase inhibition, coordination loss, and mortality. Environmental Toxicology and Chemistry. 6: 705-708.

Clark, D.R., Jr.; Alexander, J.K. 1983. DDE in brown and white fat of hibernating bats. Environmental Toxicology and Chemistry. 31: 287-299.

Clark, D.R., Jr.; Lamont, T.G. 1976. Organochlorine residues in females and nursing young of the big brown bat (*Eptesicus fuscus*). Bulletin of Environmental Contamination and Toxicology. 15: 1-8.

Cope, J.B.; Humphrey, S.R. 1972. Reproduction in the bats *Myotis keenii* and *Pipistrellus subflavus* in Indiana. Bat Research News. 13: 9-10.

Cope, J.B.; Whitaker, J.O., Jr.; Gummer, S.L. 1991. Duration of bat colonies in Indiana, USA. In: Proceedings, Indiana Academy of Science. 99: 199-202.

Creel, G.C. 1963. Bats as a food item of *Rana pipiens*. Texas Journal of Science. 15: 104.

Currie, R.R. 1999. An overview of the response of bats to protection efforts. In: Proceedings, Indiana Bat Symposium. Lexington, KY: Bat Conservation International. 24 p.

Davis, W.H. 1959a. Disproportionate sex ratios in hibernating bats. Journal of Mammalogy. 40: 16-19.

Davis, W.H. 1959b. Taxonomy of the eastern pipistrelle. Journal of Mammalogy. 40: 521-531.

Davis, W.H. 1963. Aging bats in winter. Transactions, Kentucky Academy of Science. 24: 28-30.

Davis, W.H. 1964. Winter awakening patterns in the bats *Myotis lucifugus* and *Pipistrellus subflavus*. Journal of Mammalogy. 45(4): 645-647.

Davis, W.H. 1966. Population dynamics of the bat *Pipistrellus subflavus*. Journal of Mammalogy. 47: 383-396.

Davis, W.H.; Hitchcock, H.B. 1965. Biology and migration of the bat *Myotis lucifugus* in New England. Journal of Mammalogy. 46: 296-313.

Davis, W.H.; Mumford, R.E. 1962. Ecological notes on the bat *Pipistrellus subflavus*. American Midland Naturalist. 68(2): 394-398.

Davis, W.H.; Reite, O.B. 1967. Responses of bats from temperate regions to changes in ambient temperature. Biological Bulletin. 132: 320-328.

Dunn, J.P.; Hall, J.S. 1989. Status of cave-dwelling bats in Pennsylvania, USA. Journal of the Pennsylvania Academy of Science. 63(3): 166-172.

Esher, R.J.; Wolfe, J.L.; Koch, R.B. 1980. DDT and DDE inhibition of bat brain ATPase activities. Comparative Biochemistry & Physiology—C: Comparative Pharmacology. 65(1): 43-46.

Farney, J.; Fleharty, E. 1969. Aspect ratio, loading, wing span and membrane area of bats. Journal of Mammalogy. 50: 362-367.

Feldhammer, G.A.; Carter, T.C.; Carroll, S.K. 2001. Timing of pregnancy, lactation and female foraging activity in three species of bats in southern Illinois. Canadian Field-Naturalist. 115(3): 420-424.

Fenton, M.B. 1970. Population studies of *Myotis lucifugus* in Ontario. Life Sci. Occas. Pap. Toronto, ON: Royal Ontario Museum. 77: 1-34.

Findley, J.S. 1954. Tree roosting of the eastern pipistrelle. Journal of Mammalogy. 35(3): 434-435.

Findley, J.S.; Studier, E.H.; Wilson, D.E. 1972. Morphologic properties of bat wings. Journal of Mammalogy. 53(3): 429-444.

Fitch, J.H. 1966. Weight loss and temperature response in three species of bats in Marshall County, Kansas. Search. 6: 17-24.

Forest Inventory and Analysis. 2003. Forest Inventory and Analysis. U.S. Department of Agriculture Forest Service. 98 p.

Fujita, M.S.; Kunz, T.H. 1984. *Pipistrellus subflavus*. Mammalian Species. 228: 1-6.

Geluso, K. 1976. Bat mortality: pesticide poisoning and migratory stress. Science. 194: 184-186.

Geluso, K.; Mollhagen, T.R.; Tigner, J.M.; Bogan, M.A. 2004. Westward expansion of the eastern pipistrelle (*Pipistrellus subflavus)* in the United States, including new records from New Mexico, South Dakota, and Texas. Western North American Naturalist. 65(3): 405-409.

Gillette, D.D.; Kimbrough, J.D. 1970. Chiropteran mortality. In: Slaughter, I., ed. About bats. Dallas: Southern Methodist University Press. 262-283 p.

Gould, E. 1955. The feeding efficiency of insectivorous bats. Journal of Mammalogy. 36(3): 399-407.

Greenhall, A.M.; Paradiso, J.L. 1968. Bats and bat banding. Washington, DC: U.S. Department of the Interior, Bureau of Sport Fisheries and Wildlife; U.S. Government Printing Office. 22 p.

Griffin, D.R. 1934. Marking bats. Journal of Mammalogy. 15: 202-207.

Griffin, D.R. 1936. Bat banding. Journal of Mammalogy. 17: 235-239.

Griffith, L.A.; Gates, J.E. 1985. Food habits of cave-dwelling bats in the central Appalachians. Journal of Mammalogy. 66(3): 451-460.

Guthrie, M.J. 1933. The reproductive cycles of some cave bats. Journal of Mammalogy. 14: 199-216.

Hahn, W.L. 1908. Some habits and sensory adaptations of cave inhabiting bats. Biological Bulletin. 15: 135-193.

Hall, J.S. 1962. A life history and taxonomic study of the Indiana bat, *Myotis sodalis*. Reading Public Museum and Art Gallery, Science Publication. 12: 1-68.

Hamilton, W.J.; Whitaker, J.O., Jr. 1979. Mammals of the Eastern United States. Ithaca, NY: Cornell University Press. 346 p.

Harvey, M.J. 1999. Eastern bat species of concern to mining. Unpublished paper. Cookeville, TN: Tennessee Tech University. 4 p.

Herreid, C.F. 1964. Bat longevity and metabolic rate. Experimental Gerontol. 1: 1-9.

Hitchcock, H.B. 1965. Twenty-three years of bat banding in Ontario and Quebec. Canadian Field Naturalist. 79: 4-14.

Hornacki, J.H.; Kinman, K.E.; Koeppl, J.W. 1982. Mammal species of the world: a taxonomic and geographic reference. Lawrence, KS: Allen Press. 694 p.

Hoying, K.N.; Kunz, T.H. 1998. Variation in size at birth and post-natal growth in the insectivorous bat *Pipistrellus subflavus* (Chiroptera: Vespertilionidae). Journal of Zoology London. 245(1): 15-27.

Humphrey, S.R. 1975. Nursery roosts and community diversity of neararctic bats. Journal of Mammalogy. 56: 321-346.

Humphrey, S.R. 1978. Status, winter habitat, and management of the endangered Indiana bat, *Myotis sodalis*. Florida Scientist. 41: 65-76.

Humphrey, S.R.; Cope, J.B. 1976. Population ecology of the little brown bat, *Myotis lucifugus*, in Indiana and north-central Kentucky. Spec. Pubs. American Society of Mammalogy. 4: 1-81.

Humphrey, S.R.; LaVal, R.K.; Clawson, R.L. 1976. Nursery populations of *Pipistrellus subflavus* (Chiroptera: Vespertilionidae) in Missouri. Transactions, Illinois State Academy of Science. 69(3): 367.

Jennings, W.L. 1958. The ecological distribution of bats in Florida. Gainesville, FL: University of Florida. 126 p. Ph.D. dissertation.

Johnson, B. 2001. Personal communication. Wildlife biologist, USDA Forest Service, Region 9, Milwaukee, WI.

Jones, C.; Pagels, J. 1968. Notes on a population of *Pipistrellus subflavus* in southern Louisiana. Journal of Mammalogy. 49: 134-139.

Jones, C.; Suttkus, R.D. 1973. Colony structure and organization of *Pipistrellus subflavus* in southern Louisiana. Journal of Mammalogy. 54: 962-968.

Knowles, B. 1992. Bat hibernacula on Lake Superior's North Shore, Minnesota. Canadian Field-Naturalist. 106(2): 252-254.

Krutzsch, P.H.; Crichton, E.G. 1986. Reproduction of the male pipistrelle, *Pipistrellus subflavus*, in the North-Eastern United States. Journal of Reproductive Fertility. 76: 91-104.

Kurta, A. 1982. A review of Michigan bats: seasonal and geographic distribution. Michigan Academy of Science. 14: 295-312.

Kurta, A. 2000. Personal communication. Professor of Terrestrial Ecology, Eastern Michigan University, Ypsilanti, MI.

Kurta, A. 2001. Biology and management of an endangered species. Indiana Bat Symposium; Lexington, Kentucky. Austin, TX: Bat Conservation International. 87 p.

Kurta, A.; Bell, G.P.; Nagy, K.A.; Kunz, T.H. 1989. Energetics of pregnancy and lactation in free-ranging little brown bats (*Myotis lucifugus*). Physiological Zoology. 62: 804-818.

Lacki, M.J.; Bookhout, T.A. 1983. A survey of bats in Wayne National Forest, Ohio. Ohio Journal of Science. 83(1): 45-50.

Lacki, M.J.; Hutchinson, J.T. 1999. Communities of bats (Chiroptera) in the Grayson Lake Region of northeastern Kentucky. Journal of the Kentucky Academy of Science. 60(1): 38-44.

Lane, H.K. 1946. Notes on *Pipistrellus subflavus subflavus* (F. Cuvier) during the season of parturition. Proceedings, Pennsylvania Academy of Science. 20: 57-61.

LaVal, R.K.; LaVal, M.L. 1980. Ecological studies and management of Missouri bats, with emphasis on cave-dwelling species. Missouri Department of Conservation, Terrestrial Series. 8: 19.

Lechner, A.J. 1985. Pulmonary design in a microchiropteran bat *Pipistrellus subflavus* during hibernation. Respiratory Physiology. 59(3): 301-312.

Lee, D.S.; Clark, M.K. 1993. Notes on post-breeding American swallow-tailed kites *Elanoides forficatus* in north central Florida. Brimleyana. 19: 185-203.

MacDonald, K.; Matsui, E.; Fenton, M.B.; Stevens, R. 1994. Echolocation calls and field identification of the eastern pipistrelle (*Pipistrellus subflavus*) using ultrasonic bat detectors. Journal of Mammalogy. 75(2): 462-465.

Martin, R.L. 1961. Current aspects of the U.S. rabies problem. Bat Banding News. 2: 22-26.

McNab, B.K. 1974a. The behavior of temperate cave bats in a subtropical environment. Ecology. 55: 943-958.

McNab, B.K. 1974b. The energetics of endotherms. Ohio Journal of Science. 74: 370-380.

Menu, H. 1984. Revision of the status of *Pipistrellus subflavus* (F. Cuvier, 1832). A new generic name is proposed: *Perimyotis* new genus. Mammalia. 48(3): 409-416.

Menzel, M.A.; Krishon, D.M.; Laerm, J.; Carter, T.C. 1999. Notes on tree roost characteristics of the northern yellow bat (*Lasiurus intermedius*), the Seminole bat (*L. seminolus*), and the eastern pipistrelle (*Pipistrellus subflavus*). Florida Scientist. 62: 185-193.

Miller, G.S.; Allen, G.M. 1928. The American bats of the genera *Myotis* and *Pizonyx*. Bulletin of the United States National Museum. 144: 1-218.

Mohr, C.E. 1952. A survey of bat banding in North America, 1932-1951. NSS Bulletin. 34: 33-47.

Mumford, R.E.; Cope, J.B. 1964. Distribution and status of the Chiroptera of Indiana. American Midland Naturalist. 72(2): 473-489.

Mumford, R.E.; Whitaker, J.O. 1975. Seasonal activity of bats at an Indiana cave. In: Proceedings, Indiana Academy of Science. 84: 500-507.

Myers, R.F. 1964. Ecology of three species of myotine bats in the Ozark Plateau. Columbia, MO: University of Missouri. 250 p. Ph.D. dissertation.

NatureServe. 2002. NatureServe Explorer: an online encyclopedia of life [Web application]. Version 4.1. http://www.natureserve.org.

Nickel, P.A.; Hansen, M.F. 1967. Helminths of bats collected in Kansas, Nebraska, and Oklahoma. The American Midland Naturalist. 78: 481-486.

Norberg, U.M. 1981. Allometry of bat wings and legs and comparison with bird wings. Philosophical Transactions, Royal Society of London. 287: 131-165.

Norberg, U.M. 1986. Evolutionary convergence in foraging niche and flight morphology in insectivores and aerial hawking birds and bats. Orn Scand. 17: 253-260.

Norberg, U.M.; Raynor, J.M.V. 1987. Ecological morphology and flight in bats (Mammalia; Chiroptera): wing adaptations, flight performance, foraging strategy and echolocation. Philosophical Transactions, Royal Society of London. 316: 335-427.

Orr, R.T. 1970. Development: prenatal and postnatal. In: Wimsatt, W.A., ed. Biology of bats. New York: Academic Press: 217-231.

O'Shea, T.J.; Clark, D.R., Jr. 2001. Overview of impacts of contaminants on bats: with special reference to the Indiana bat. Bat Research News. 42: 36.

Paradiso, J.L. 1969. Mammals of Maryland. North American Fauna. 66: 1-193.

Paradiso, J.L.; Greenhall, A.M. 1966. Longevity records for American bats. American Midland Naturalist. 78: 251.

Ploskey, G.R.; Sealer, J.A. 1979. Lipid deposition and withdrawal before and during hibernation in *Pipistrellus subflavus*. Southwestern Naturalist. 24(1): 71-78.

Powell, V.N. 1983. Industrial effluents as a source of mercury contamination in terrestrial riparian vertebrates. Environmental Pollution, Series B: Chemical & Physical. 5(1): 51-58.

Rabinowitz, A. 1981. Thermal preference of the eastern pipistrelle bat (*Pipistrellus subflavus*) during hibernation. Journal of the Tennessee Academy of Science. 56: 113-114.

Reidinger, R.F., Jr. 1976. Organochlorine residues in adults of six southwestern bat species. Journal of Wildlife Management. 40: 677-680.

Reidinger, R.F., Jr.; Cockrum, E.L. 1978. Organochlorine residues in free-tailed bats (*Tadarida brasiliensis*) at Eagle Creek Cave, Greenlee County, Arizona. In: Proceedings, Fourth International Bat Research Conference. Nairobi, Kenya: Kenya Literature Bureau: 85-96.

Rysgaard, G. 1941. A study of the cave bats of Minnesota with especial reference to the large brown bat. East Lansing, MI: Michigan State College. 64 p. M.S. thesis.

Sandel, J.K.; Benatar, G.R.; Walker, C.W.; Burke, K.M.; Lacher, T.E.; Honeycutt, R.L. 2001. Use and selection of winter hibernacula by the eastern pipistrelle (*Pipistrellus subflavus*) in Texas. Journal of Mammalogy. 82(1): 173-178.

Sanders, W. 2000. Dorset (Mt. Aeolus) Cave Greeley talc mine trapping report. Report to U.S. Fish & Wildlife Service. Burlington, VT: [Publisher unknown]. 3 p.

Schmidly, D.J.; Wilkens, K.T.; Weyn, B.C.; Honeycutt, R.L. 1977. The bats of east Texas. Texas Journal of Science. 28: 127-143.

Sheffield, S.R.; Chapman, B.R. 1992. First records of mammals from McCurtain County, Oklahoma. Texas Journal of Science. 44: 491-492.

Speakman, J.; Racey, P.A.; Webb, P.I.; Catto, C.M.C.; Swift, S.M.; Burnett, A.M. 1991. Minimum summer populations and densities of bats in N.E. Scotland, near the northern borders of their distributions. Journal of Zoology London. 225: 327-345.

Stevenson, D.; Tuttle, M.D. 1982. Growth and survival of bats. In: Kunz, T.H., ed. Ecology of bats. New York: Plenum. 425 p.

Tibbels, A.B.; Kurta, A. 2003. Bat activity is low in thinned and unthinned stands of red pine. Canada Journal of Forest Restoration. 33: 2436-2442.

Trombulak, S.C.; Higuera, P.E.; DesMeules, M. 2001. Population trends of wintering bats in Vermont. Northeastern Naturalist. 8: 51-62.

Tuttle, M.D. 1979. Status, causes of decline, and management of endangered gray bats. Journal of Wildlife Management. 43: 1-17.

Tuttle, M.D. 1981. Gating as a means of protecting cave dwelling bats. In: Stitt, R., ed. Cage gating; a handbook. 2nd ed., rev. Huntsville, AL: National Speleological Society: 40-45.

Unger, C.A.; Kurta, A. 1998. Status of the eastern pipistrelle (Mammalia: Chiroptera) in Michigan. Michigan Academician. 30: 423-437.

Veilleux, J.P. 2001. Tree roosting ecology of reproductive female eastern pipistrelles, *Pipistrellus subflavus*. Bat Research News. 42: 80.

Veilleux, J.P.; Whitaker, J.O., Jr.; Veilleux, S.L. 2003. Tree-roosting ecology of reproductive female eastern pipistrelles, *Pipistrellus subflavus*, in Indiana. Journal of Mammalogy. 84(3): 1068-1075.

Walley, H.D.; Jarvis, W.L. 1971. Longevity record for *Pipistrellus subflavus*. Illinois Academy of Science. 64: 305.

Whitaker, J.O. 1972. Food habits of bats from Indiana. Canadian Journal of Zoology. 50: 877-883.

Whitaker, J.O. 1998. Life history and roost switching in six summer colonies of eastern pipistrelles in buildings. Journal of Mammalogy. 79(2): 651-659.

Whitaker, J.O.; Loomis, R.B. 1979. Chiggers from the mammals of Indiana. In: Proceedings, Indiana Academy of Science. 88: 426-433.

Whitaker, J.O.; Mumford, R.E. 1973. External parasites of bats of Indiana. The Journal of Parasitology. 59: 1148-1150.

Whitaker, J.O.; Rissler, L.J. 1992. Winter activity of bats at a mine entrance in Vermillion County, Indiana. American Midland Naturalist. 127: 52-59.

Whitaker, J.O.; Stacy, M. 1996. Bats of abandoned coal mines in southwestern Indiana. In: Proceedings, Indiana Academy of Science. 105: 277-280.

Williamson, A. 2001. Personal communication. Wildlife
Biologist, USDA Forest Service, Region 9, Milwaukee, WI.
Phone conversation.

Wimsatt, W.A. 1945. Notes on breeding behavior, pregnancy
and parturition in some vespertilionid bats in the Eastern
United States. Journal of Mammalogy. 26: 23-33.

Winchell, J.M.; Kunz, T.H. 1996. Day-roosting activity budgets
of the eastern pipistrelle bat, *Pipistrellus subflavus* (Chiroptera:
Vespertilionidae). Canadian Journal of Zoology. 74(3): 431-441.

Conservation Assessment: *Nycticeius humeralis* (Evening Bat) in the Eastern United States

Sybill Amelon[1] **and Dirk Burhans**[2]

Taxonomy and Nomenclature

The evening bat or evening myotis [*Nycticeius humeralis* (Rafinesque 1818) (f. L. *nycticeius* belonging to the night; *humeralis* pertaining to the humerus)] belongs to the class Mammalia, order Chiroptera, family Vespertilionidae, subfamily Vespertilioninae, genus/species *Nycticeius humeralis* (Rafinesque 1818). Other common names include twilight bat and black-shouldered bat. The genus *Nycticeius* includes 14 species; but only two of these species are native to the New World (Watkins 1972).

Three subspecies of *N. humeralis* are recognized (Hall and Kelson 1959):

1. *N. h. humeralis* = *Vespertilio humeralis* (Rafinesque 1818: 445). Type location is Kentucky. = *Nycticea crepuscularis* (Le Conte in [McMurtrie 1831: 432]). Type location is not stated.
2. *N. h. mexicanus* (Davis 1944: 380). Type location is Rio Ramos, Nuevo Leon, Mexico.
3. *N. h. subtropicalis* (Schwartz 1951: 233). Type location is Monroe Station, Collier County, Florida.

Description of Species

N. humeralis is a medium-sized bat that resembles a small big brown bat (*Eptesicus fuscus*), but its much shorter forearm and single upper incisors distinguish it from *E. fuscus*. Characteristic measurements include wingspan, 260 to 280 millimeters (mm); total length, 88 to 105 mm; tail length, 36 to 41 mm; hindfoot, 6 to 9 mm; ear, 11 to 15 mm, thick and leathery; forearm, 34 to 38 mm; and skull, short and broad with a nearly straight dorsal profile. Weight ranges from 5 to 14 grams (g). Females are consistently heavier than males. Pelage color dorsally varies from dull, medium brown to dark brown; ventrally, the fur is lighter. Hairs are short and very dark near the base. Juvenile pelage is darker than adult pelage. The tragus is short and rounded. The dental formula is i 1/3, c 1/1, p 1/2, m 3/3, total 30. A characteristic feature of this species is the presence of a single upper incisor (Hamilton and Whitaker 1979, Watkins 1972).

Biology, Life History, and Natural History

Reproductive Biology and Phenology

The reproductive cycle of *N. humeralis* is not well known. Evening bats are polygamous, with breeding activity occurring in the fall and potentially into spring (Bain and Humphrey 1986). In Florida, mating apparently begins in October and occurs throughout the winter (Bain and Humphrey 1986). Sperm are stored in the uterus of hibernating females until spring ovulation (Guthrie 1933).

In northwest Missouri, the earliest reported captures in the year were in late April and early May (Easterla and Watkins 1970, Watkins 1970). At a colony in Montgomery County, IN, Humphrey and Cope (1968) observed 2, 42, 106, and 159 *N. humeralis* on May 1, 7, 14, and 21, respectively. Adult males and females segregate at least in spring and summer (Jones 1967).

In Florida, young were born synchronously in late May (Bain and Humphrey 1986). In northern Missouri, females gave birth by mid-June (Watkins and Shump 1981). All palpitated females had twins, although one gave birth to triplets after capture (Bain and Humphrey 1986). Watkins (1970) found an average of 1.9 embryos out of 87 bats collected from April 19 to July 8. Additional information collected by Watkins (1970)

[1] Wildlife biologist, U.S. Department of Agriculture, Forest Service, North Central Research Station, Columbia, MO.

[2] Postdoctoral associate, Department of Fisheries and Wildlife Science, University of Missouri, Columbia, MO.

indicates a high percentage of females with three embryos. In Alabama and Louisiana, births occur from mid-May to mid-June. Young are born hairless and pink with eyes closed; eyes open 12 to 30 hours later. Short fur can be detected at 5 days of age (Jones 1967). Newborn *N. humeralis* are capable of making loud clicking sounds that may aid their mothers in retrieving them (Jones and Genoways 1967). Growth rates vary by type of roost and geographic location (Jones and Pagels 1968). Young become volant in approximately 3 weeks (Bain and Humphrey 1986, Watkins 1970, Wilkinson 1992). Sex ratios have been reported as equal among offspring, skewed to females as juveniles, and nearly equal for adults (Humphrey and Cope 1970). Juvenile males were reproductively mature at less than 1 month old (Bain and Humphrey 1986). Males generally disperse from natal roosts, whereas females remain until southern migration (Bain and Humphrey 1986, Watkins and Shump 1981).

Ecology and Behavior

In northern Missouri, southern migration of *N. humeralis* began in mid-September (Watkins and Shump 1981). October 11 and 20 were the last dates bats were found at colonies in Missouri and Iowa, respectively (Easterla and Watkins 1970). Humphrey and Cope (1968) noted reductions from 275 to 30 individuals from August 15 to September 21, respectively, at a colony in Montgomery County, IN.

The absence of *N. humeralis* in the northern extent of its range during winter strongly suggests that it migrates. Humphrey and Cope (1970) found several individuals 176 to 547 kilometers (km) south of their summer locations. Autumn fat deposition indicates this species prepares for long migrations and/or hibernation (Baker 1968). Evening bats are rarely known to use caves. They have been found to use tree hollows during winter (Duchamp 2000).

Maternity colonies have been reported in trees, buildings, and other human-made structures (Clem 1992, Cope and Humphrey 1967, Humphrey and Cope 1970). Sexes are segregated during the maternity period; females remain in small maternity colonies and males remain solitary (Clem 1992).

Of 19 *N. humeralis* monitored in Indiana, only three made more than one foraging trip per night; all three were lactating females (Clem 1993). Post-lactating females foraged for the longest bouts (mean = 127.4 minutes [min]), followed by lactating females (mean = 107.2 min) and pregnant females (mean = 78.3 min) (Clem 1993). *N. humeralis* does not appear to have exclusive feeding territories; in 38 percent of 80 monitored flights, two or more bats fed in the same area at the same time (Clem 1993). Obligate associations with other species have not been observed. *N. humeralis* has been observed roosting with big brown bats.

Of nursing bouts monitored by Wilkinson (1992), 18 percent involved females nursing nondescendant offspring that tended to be females. He proposed that adult females benefited by dumping excess milk and that favoring female young helps increase colony size because male offspring tend to disperse.

In open habitats, *N. humeralis* produce 7 millisecond, frequency modulated/constant frequency (FM/CF) echolocation calls. Minimum frequency is typically 34 to 36 kilohertz (kHz), and maximum frequency is typically 47 to 50 kHz.

Hibernation

Little is known about the hibernation behavior of *N. humeralis*. The species has only occasionally been observed at mine or cave entrances during swarming activities in the fall. Anecdotal information suggests this species spends the winter in tree cavities or buildings in the southern regions of its range. *N. humeralis* is believed to be active during warm periods in the winter.

Food Habits

N. humeralis has been reported feeding on coleopterans and hemipterans (Whitaker 1972). In a study of guano pellets in Indiana (Whitaker and Clem 1992), beetles, moths, and leaf hoppers were reported to be the main foods that evening bats ate; the spotted cucumber beetle (*Diabrotica undecimpunctata*), an agricultural pest, was the species the bats took most frequently (14.2 percent of total volume). Carter et al. (1998) found that *N. humeralis* feed on coleopterans and hymenopterans in Georgia.

Mortality and Predation Factors

Whitaker et al. (1991) stated that two mites (*Steatonyssus ceratognathus* and *Acanthophthirius nycticeius*) and the bat bug (*Cimex adjunctus*) were the only ectoparasites infesting *N. humeralis* throughout its range. Endoparasites include nematodes (Watkins 1970, 1972). Predators of *N. humeralis* include humans, cats, raccoons, snakes, and birds of prey.

Longevity

The greatest observed longevity for *N. humeralis* is 5 years (Watkins 1972).

Banding Data and Site Fidelity

Based on early banding records, the maximum distance *N. humeralis* travels is 547 km in the fall (Cope and Humphrey 1967). Homing studies found that individuals would return to their original capture sites from distances of up to 153 km (Cope and Humphrey 1967).

Distribution

In summer, *N. humeralis* occurs in at least small numbers as far north as New Jersey, Pennsylvania, southern Michigan, and Illinois, but reaches its maximum numbers in the South, where it is found as far west as Kansas and eastern Texas and as far south as northern Veracruz, Mexico; it is thought to be absent from the Appalachians (Hamilton and Whitaker 1979) (fig. 1).

Figure 1. *The distribution of* Nycticeius humeralis.

* = Isolated or questionable records.
Source: Bat Conservation International 2003, http://www.batcon.org.

Habitat Requirements

Maternity Period (May to August)

Roosting Habitat
Menzel et al. (1999) found *N. humeralis* roosting in slash pine, loblolly pine, and live oak. The preferred tree species was oak. Before 1993, all the *N. humeralis* maternity colonies known from Indiana were located in buildings; between 1960 and 1993, 11 colonies in buildings were abandoned (Whitaker et al. 2002). In 1994, researchers studied a maternity colony in Vigo County, IN, where evening bats were using hollows in silver maples as roosting sites. These silver maples were located in a 650-hectare (ha) bottom-land hardwood forest. Females were found to switch roosts frequently, even when pups were present. The number of females fluctuated greatly at specific trees on a given night. When young become volant, movement between trees increases. In South Carolina, Menzel et al. (2001) found 13 of 14 roosts used by three adult female *N. humeralis* in cavities of upland longleaf pine sawtimber stands characterized by open canopies. The mean number of days between roost changes was 2.3. The remaining roost was under the exfoliating bark of a live longleaf pine. Roosts have been located in Spanish moss (Jennings 1958) and under exfoliating bark (Chapman and Chapman 1990, Menzel et al. 2000).

Foraging Habitat
Female *N. humeralis* bats in Indiana were found to forage in association with their roosts in bottom-land forests (Whitaker and Gummer 2003). *N. humeralis* in South Carolina foraged over riparian zones, over beaver ponds, and in gaps in bottom-land hardwood and swamp forests (Menzel et al. 2001). Attic temperatures below 13 °C decreased foraging activity of bats in an Indiana bell tower, and colonies emerged later after sunset as the breeding season progressed (Clem 1993).

    N. humeralis is believed to intermittently forage from dusk to midnight and then have another period of feeding activity toward dawn.

Hibernation Period (October to April)

Whitaker and Gummer (1993) suggested that *N. humeralis* moves south during winter and hibernates in tree holes near major rivers. They based their findings on recaptures of individuals that were banded in Indiana and later found in Kentucky. In southern portions of their range, *N. humeralis* has been found in buildings and hollow trees during winter.

Potential Threats

Natural or Human Factors

Bat population declines have been attributed to pesticide poisoning (Geluso 1976, Reidinger 1976), chemical pollution (Tuttle 1979), siltation of waterways (Tuttle 1979), flooding (Hall 1962), and disturbance by humans (Fenton 1970, Humphrey 1978, Tuttle 1979, Speakman et al. 1991). Food chain poisoning by pesticides—in particular insecticides such as organochlorines and anticholinesterase—has been demonstrated to negatively affect insectivorous bats (Clark 2001, Cockrum 1970, Reidinger and Cockrum 1978, Clark et al. 1983).

Because *N. humeralis* bats often use buildings, Whitaker and Gummer (1993) considered them highly sensitive to disturbances by humans and less tolerant of human disturbance than were big brown bats (*E. fuscus*), a species that will relocate to a new roost after evictions. Bain (1981) indicated that excessive disturbance to a nursing colony caused abandonment. A colony in a church bell tower declined by 49 percent in 1990 after 1989 banding and radiotelemetry studies (Clem 1992). Watkins (1970) stated that evening bats abandoned six northwestern Missouri colonies in reaction to his survey and netting operations, although other colonies persisted despite disturbance.

Present or Potential Risks to Habitat

The evening bat is a species whose range coincides with the historic extent of large river valleys, lowland swamps, and the wetlands characteristic of the Southeastern United States and the Mississippi and Ohio River Valleys. Although minimal data are available on historic habitat use, current studies and

anecdotal reports strongly suggest this species may have been associated with bottom-land forests, swamps, and wetlands.

Realistic estimates of the original extent of lowland forest and wetlands are not available because accurate records of these types were not maintained until the early 20th century, and many accounts of wetland size were little more than speculation (Hefner and Brown 1985). Hayes and Klopatek (1979) estimated that the precolonial forested wetland area of the United States was about 27.2 million ha (67.2 million acres).

Although current estimates of lowland forest and wetlands area vary, it has been estimated that as of the mid-1950s the United States had about 19.1 million ha (47.2 million acres) of forested wetlands. The estimated area of southern bottom-land hardwoods declined to 12.5 to 13.1 million ha (30.9 to 32.4 million acres) by the mid-1970s (Hefner and Brown 1985). By the mid-1980s, an additional 1.4 million ha (3.5 million acres) of lowland forest and wetlands were lost, mostly from the Southeastern United States.

The most dramatic bottom-land hardwood loss in the entire Nation has occurred in the Lower Mississippi River region. This vast area extends nearly 1,000 km (621 miles) from the confluence of the Mississippi and Ohio Rivers to the Gulf of Mexico; it originally covered more than 10.1 million ha (25.0 million acres) (Hefner and Brown 1985). Recent estimates reveal that fewer than 2 million ha (4.9 million acres) of lowland forest and wetlands remain in the lower Mississippi River region, and the remaining portions of the original area are extremely fragmented.

Inadequacy of Existing Regulatory Mechanisms

Protection of natural and human-made roosting structures is one of the highest priorities for conservation of *N. humeralis*. Funding to facilitate protection measures is often unavailable.

Population Status

Rangewide

Both Global Heritage Status and National Heritage Status are very common—G5, N5 (NatureServe 2002)—indicating the *N. humeralis* is globally and nationally demonstrably widespread and common.

State

Individual State Heritage Status is described in the State Summaries and in table 1. *N. humeralis* is believed to be most common in the southern parts of its range. Systematic, uniform population surveys have not been routinely conducted; population data are fairly scarce; and concerns of accuracy exist among areas and sampling methods. Demographic information on reproductive rates, sex ratios, movement between roosting sites, movement between maternity roosts and winter roosts, recruitment, and reproduction is necessary to provide a quantitative estimate of population viability.

Habitat Status

Summary of Land Ownership and Existing Habitat Protection

National Forests

Estimates of the potential available habitat for *N. humeralis* were based on U.S. Department of Agriculture (USDA) Forest Service Forest Inventory and Analysis (FIA) data, which estimates the amount of upland hardwood and pine-hardwood forest land more than 60 years old for all States with national forests in Regions 8 and 9 (Southern and Eastern Forest Service Regions combined to look at the entire species range) and Region 9 (examined alone to look at potential available habitat for States in Region 9), excluding rarely used deciduous forest types such as aspen. This coarse-scale assessment of habitat availability considers forest type and age class based on FIA data (USDA 2003). This analysis does not consider other aspects of forest structure that may influence use by this species. The database used is subject to sampling errors associated with coarse-scale inventory. Estimates were for the acreage of upland hardwood and pine-hardwood forest land for forests of all ownerships, including other federally owned, State-owned, county/municipal-owned, and privately owned lands within these States. Approximately 5.9 percent of upland hardwood, bottom-land hardwood, and pine-hardwood forest types occur on National Forest System (NFS) lands within the range of this species; 2.9 percent occur on NFS lands within Region 9 (figs. 2 and 5). Estimates indicate that

Figure 2. *Ownership of upland hardwood, bottom-land hardwood, and pine-hardwood forest types within States overlapping the range of* N. humeralis.

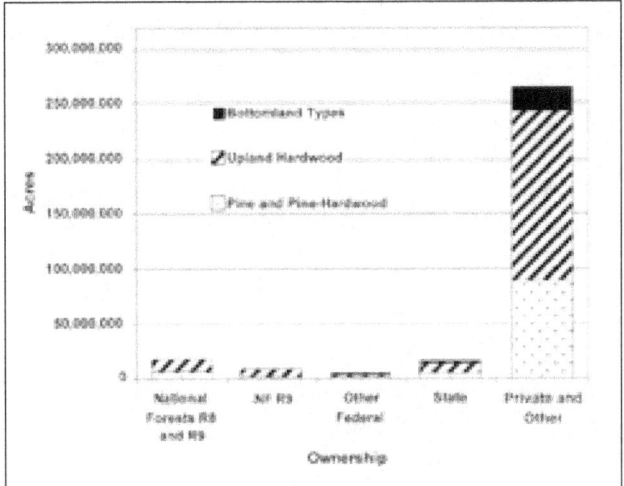

Alabama, Arkansas, Connecticut, Delaware, Florida, Georgia, Illinois, Indiana, Iowa, Kansas, Kentucky, Louisiana, Maine, Massachusetts, Michigan, Minnesota, Mississippi, Missouri, Nebraska, New Hampshire, New Jersey, New York, North Carolina, Ohio, Oklahoma, Pennsylvania, Rhode Island, South Carolina, Tennessee, Texas, Vermont, Virginia, West Virginia, Wisconsin.

358,219,772 potential acres of upland hardwood, bottom-land hardwood, and pine-hardwood forest land that could potentially serve as foraging habitat occur within the range of this species. Estimates also indicate that stands more than 60 years old in upland hardwood and pine-hardwood forest types would provide suitable trees to meet this species' roosting requirements. Within the range of this species, estimates indicate that 304,486,806 acres occur and 94,453,427 acres, or 31 percent of the total available, are more than 60 years old (figs. 3 and 4). On NFS lands within Region 9, estimates indicate 9,671,251 acres of potential foraging habitat (upland hardwood, bottom-land hardwood, and pine-hardwood forest types) and 3,786,768 acres of upland hardwood, bottom-land hardwood, and pine-hardwood forest types more than 60 years old (39.3 percent) available for roosting (figs. 3 and 4).

State Summaries

Illinois. State status is rare to uncommon (S3, table 1). Mist-net surveys at 41 sites within the Shawnee National Forest during the summers of 1999 and 2000 resulted in the capture of 417

Figure 3. *Acreage by ownership of upland hardwood forest type and percentage of upland hardwood forest type more than 60 years old by ownership within States overlapping the range of* N. humeralis.

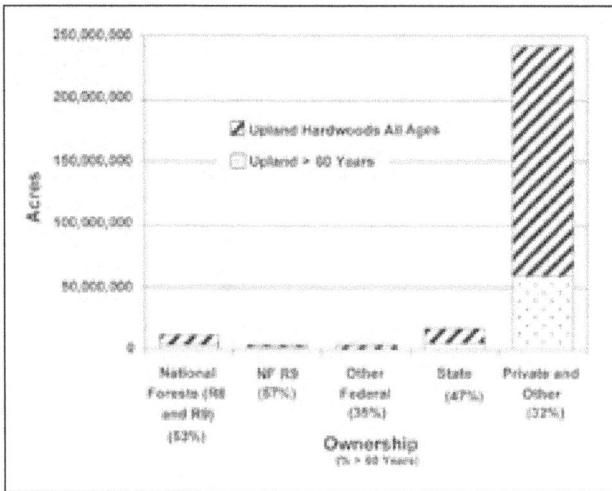

Alabama, Arkansas, Connecticut, Delaware, Florida, Georgia, Illinois, Indiana, Iowa, Kansas, Kentucky, Louisiana, Maine, Massachusetts, Michigan, Minnesota, Mississippi, Missouri, Nebraska, New Hampshire, New Jersey, New York, North Carolina, Ohio, Oklahoma, Pennsylvania, Rhode Island, South Carolina, Tennessee, Texas, Vermont, Virginia, West Virginia, Wisconsin.

Figure 4. *Acreage by ownership of pine and pine-hardwood forest types and percentage of pine and pine-hardwood forest types more than 60 years old by ownership within States overlapping the range of* N. humeralis.

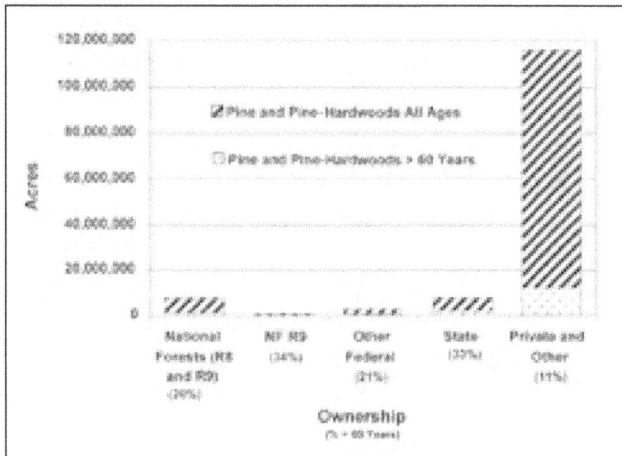

Alabama, Arkansas, Connecticut, Delaware, Florida, Georgia, Illinois, Indiana, Iowa, Kansas, Kentucky, Louisiana, Maine, Massachusetts, Michigan, Minnesota, Mississippi, Missouri, Nebraska, New Hampshire, New Jersey, New York, North Carolina, Ohio, Oklahoma, Pennsylvania, Rhode Island, South Carolina, Tennessee, Texas, Vermont, Virginia, West Virginia, Wisconsin.

bats of 10 species. *N. humeralis* were caught most frequently in forested habitats.

Indiana. State status is extremely rare; usually five or fewer occurrences in the State (S1, table1). *N. humeralis* is State-listed Endangered. All 12 *N. humeralis* colonies visited in 1959 were no longer active in the 1980s (Cope et al. 1991, Whittaker and Gummer 1993); six of the buildings containing colonies were demolished, two colonies were evicted, and three colonies left after buildings were remodeled. A single remaining colony of 358 bats was discovered in a church bell tower in 1987 during an extensive statewide survey (Whitaker and Gummer 1988).

Whitaker and Gummer believe that Indiana populations had declined based on declining numbers of historic colonies, lack of new colonies, and decreases in reported cases of rabies in *N. humeralis* (Whitaker and Gummer 1993). They also speculated that *N. humeralis* does not compete successfully with big brown bats for roosts in buildings (Whitaker and Weeks 2001). Previously unknown populations were recently

Figure 5. *Acreage by ownership of bottom-land hardwood forest type and percentage of bottom-land hardwood forest type more than 60 years old by ownership within States overlapping the range of* N. humeralis.

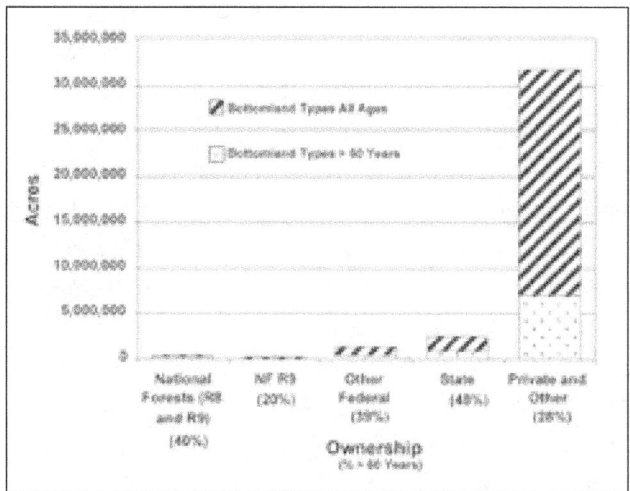

Alabama, Arkansas, Connecticut, Delaware, Florida, Georgia, Illinois, Indiana, Iowa, Kansas, Kentucky, Louisiana, Maine, Massachusetts, Michigan, Minnesota, Mississippi, Missouri, Nebraska, New Hampshire, New Jersey, New York, North Carolina, Ohio, Oklahoma, Pennsylvania, Rhode Island, South Carolina, Tennessee, Texas, Vermont, Virginia, West Virginia, Wisconsin.

Table 1. *Population status of* Nycticeius humeralis *by State.*[1]

State	Status[2]	Summer habitat (reported)	Winter habitat (reported)
Alabama	S5		Buildings
Arkansas	S3		Buildings and trees
Delaware	SNR/SU		
Florida	SNR/SU		
Georgia	S5	At forest edges, over forest canopy, and over bodies of water	Buildings, trees, and clumps of Spanish moss
Illinois	S3		Buildings and trees
Indiana	S1	Buildings and trees	Buildings and trees
Iowa	S3		
Kansas	S3, S4	Rocky areas, in buildings, and trees	Buildings and trees
Kentucky	S2, S3	Hollow trees and buildings; in forest understory, along stream corridors, and along woodland edges	Buildings and trees
Louisiana	S5		
Mississippi	S5		
Missouri	SNR/SU	Buildings, trees, and rock crevices	Buildings and trees
Nebraska	S3		
New Hampshire	NA		
New Jersey	SNR/SU		
North Carolina	S5B		
Ohio	SNR/SU		
Oklahoma	S4	Forests and woodlands	Buildings and trees
Pennsylvania	SNR/SU	Trees	Buildings and trees
South Carolina	SNR/SU		
Tennessee	S5		
Texas	S5	Forested streams	Buildings and trees
Virginia	S4		
West Virginia	S1		Buildings and trees

[1] Information about population and habitat use is based on literature cited. See text and References section.

[2] Status based on Natural Heritage State Rarity ranks (NatureServe 2002). S1: Extremely rare; usually 5 or fewer occurrences in the State, or, in the case of communities, covering less than 50 hectares (ha) in aggregate; or may have a few remaining individuals; often especially vulnerable to extirpation. S2: Very rare; usually between 5 and 20 occurrences, or, in the case of communities, covering less than 250 ha in aggregate; or few occurrences with many individuals; often susceptible to becoming endangered. S3: Rare to uncommon; usually between 20 and 100 occurrences; may have fewer occurrences, but with a large number of individuals in some populations; may be susceptible to large-scale disturbances. S4: Common; usually more than 100 occurrences, but may be fewer with many large populations; may be restricted to only a portion of the State; usually not susceptible to immediate threats. S5: Very common; secure under present conditions. SNR/SU: Status not ranked/Status uncertain, often because of low search effort or cryptic nature of the element.

discovered during netting surveys in the Prairie Creek area of Vigo County, IN (Whitaker and Gummer 2001). The authors believe the species is relatively common on the floodplain of the lower Wabash River, a large undeveloped floodplain (Sparks et al. 1998, Whitaker and Gummer 2001).

Michigan. State status: NA. The range of *N. humeralis* is believed not to include Michigan.

Minnesota. State status: NA. The range of *N. humeralis* is believed not to include Minnesota.

Missouri. State status is undetermined (SNR/SU, table 1). Watkins (1970) found 28 colonies in northwest Missouri and adjacent Iowa and estimated that 12 colonies had fewer than 100 individuals and 5 had more than 200; he estimated that 1 of the latter contained 950 bats. *N. humeralis* was the most common of eight bat species surveyed in northwest Missouri and adjacent Iowa in the late 1960s (Watkins 1970).

New Hampshire. State status: NA. The range of *N. humeralis* is believed not to include New Hampshire.

Ohio. State status is undetermined (SNR/SU, table 1). Distribution and activity of bats on the Wayne National Forest were studied in the summer and winter of 1979 and 1980. Surveys were conducted at abandoned mines and riparian sites; *N. humeralis* was not recorded in the surveys (Lacki and Bookhout 1983).

Pennsylvania. State status is undetermined (SNR/SU, table 1).

Vermont. State status: NA. The range of *N. humeralis* is believed not to include Vermont.

West Virginia. State status is extremely rare; usually five or fewer occurrences in the State (S1, table1).

Wisconsin. State status: NA. The range of *N. humeralis* is believed not to include Wisconsin.

References

Bain, J.R. 1981. Roosting ecology of three Florida bats: *Nycticeius humeralis, Myotis austroriparius, Tadarida brasiliensis*. Gainesville, FL: University of Florida. 88 p. M.S. thesis.

Bain, J.R.; Humphrey, S.R. 1986. Social organization and biased primary sex ratio of the evening bat, *Nycticeius humeralis*. Florida Scientist. 49(1): 22-31.

Baker, W.W. 1968. Autumn fat deposition in the evening bat. Journal of Mammalogy. 49: 314-317.

Carter, T.C.; Menzel, M.A.; Warnell, D.B.; Krishon, D.M.; Laerm, J. 1998. Prey selection by five species of vespertilionid bats on Sapelo Island, Georgia. Brimleyana. 25: 158-170.

Chapman, S.S.; Chapman, B.R. 1990. Bats from the coastal region of southern Texas. Texas Journal of Science. 42(1): 13-22.

Clark, D.R.; Bunck, C.M.; Cromartie, E.; LaVal, R.K. 1983. Year and age effects on residues of dieldrin and heptachlor in dead gray bats, Franklin County, Missouri—1976, 1977, and 1978. Environmental Toxicology and Chemistry. 2: 387-393.

Clark, D.R., Jr. 2001. DDT and the decline of free-tailed bats (*Tadarida brasiliensis*) at Carlsbad Caverns, New Mexico. Archives of Environmental Contamination and Toxicology. 40: 537-543.

Clem, P.D. 1992. Seasonal population variation and emergence patterns in the evening bat, *Nycticeius humeralis*, at a west-central Indiana colony. In: Proceedings, Indiana Academy of Science. 101: 33-44.

Clem, P.D. 1993. Foraging patterns and the use of temporary roosts in female evening bats, *Nycticeius humeralis*, at an Indiana maternity colony. In: Proceedings, Indiana Academy of Science. 102: 201-206.

Cockrum, E.L. 1970. Insecticides and guano bats. Ecology. 51: 761-762.

Cope, J.B.; Humphrey, S.R. 1967. Homing experiments with the evening bat, *Nycticeius humeralis*. Journal of Mammalogy. 48(1): 136.

Cope, J.B.; Whitaker, J.O., Jr.; Gummer, S.L. 1991. Duration of bat colonies in Indiana, USA. In: Proceedings, Indiana Academy of Science. 99: 199-202.

Duchamp, J. 2000. Habitat use by the evening bat, *Nycticeius humeralis*, and the big brown bat, *Eptesicus fuscus*, in Indiana. Bat Research News. 41: 115.

Easterla, D.A.; Watkins, L.C. 1970. Nursery colonies of evening bats (*Nycticeius humeralis*) in northwestern Missouri and southwestern Iowa. Transactions, Missouri Academy of Science. 4: 110-117.

Fenton, M.B. 1970. Population studies of *Myotis lucifugus* in Ontario. Life Sci. Occas. Pap. Toronto, ON: Royal Ontario Museum. 77: 1-34.

Geluso, K. 1976. Bat mortality: pesticide poisoning and migratory stress. Science. 194: 184-186.

Guthrie, M.J. 1933. The reproductive cycles of some cave bats. Journal of Mammalogy. 14: 199-216.

Hall, E.R.; Kelson, K.R. 1959. The mammals of North America. New York: Ronald Press. 1083 p.

Hall, J.S. 1962. A life history and taxonomic study of the Indiana bat, *Myotis sodalis*. Reading Public Museum and Art Gallery, Science Publication. 12: 1-68.

Hamilton, W.J.; Whitaker, J.O., Jr. 1979. Mammals of the Eastern United States. Ithaca, NY: Cornell University Press. 346 p.

Haynes, R.J.; Klopatek, J.M. 1979. Reclamation of abandoned mine lands and fish and wildlife mitigation needs. In: Mitigation symposium: a national workshop on mitigating losses of fish and wildlife habitats. Gen. Tech. Report RM-65.

Fort Collins, CO: U.S. Department of Agriculture, Forest Service, Rocky Mountain Forest and Range Experiment Station: 256-263.

Hefner, J.M.; Brown, J.D. 1985. Wetland trends in the Southeastern United States. Wetlands. 4: 1-11.

Humphrey, S.R. 1978. Status, winter habitat, and management of the endangered Indiana bat, *Myotis sodalis*. Florida Scientist. 41: 65-76.

Humphrey, S.R.; Cope, J.B. 1968. Records of migration of the evening bat, *Nycticeius humeralis*. Journal of Mammalogy. 49(2): 329.

Humphrey, S.R.; Cope, J.B. 1970. Population samples of the evening bat, *Nycticeius humeralis*. Journal of Mammalogy. 51(2): 399-401.

Jennings, W.L. 1958. The ecological distribution of bats in Florida. Gainesville, FL: University of Florida. 126 p. Ph.D. dissertation.

Jones, C. 1967. Growth development and wing loading in the evening bat *Nycticeius humeralis*. Journal of Mammalogy. 48: 1-19.

Jones, C.; Pagels, J. 1968. Notes on a population of *Pipistrellus subflavus* in southern Louisiana. Journal of Mammalogy. 49: 134-139.

Jones, J.K.; Genoways, H.H. 1967. Annotated checklist of bats from South Dakota. Transactions of the Kansas Academy of Science. 70: 184-196.

Lacki, M.J.; Bookhout, T.A. 1983. A survey of bats in Wayne National Forest, Ohio. Ohio Journal of Science. 83(1): 45-50.

McMurtrie, H. 1831. The animal kingdom arranged in conformity with its organization. Trans. H. McMurtrie, by the Baron Cuvier translated from French. New York. Vol. 4.

Menzel, M.A.; Carter, T.C.; Chapman, B.R.; Ford, W.M. 2001. Tree-roost characteristics of subadult and female adult evening bats (*Nycticeius humeralis*) in the Upper Coastal Plain of South Carolina. American Midland Naturalist. 145: 112-119.

Menzel, M.A.; Carter, T.C.; Ford, W.M.; Chapman, B.R.; Ozier, J. 2000. Summer roost tree selection by eastern red, Seminole, and evening bats in the Upper Coast Plain of South Carolina. Proceedings of the Annual Conference of the Southeastern Association of Fish and Wildlife Agencies. 54: 304-313.

Menzel, M.A.; Krishon, D.M.; Laerm, J.; Carter, T.C. 1999. Notes on tree roost characteristics of the northern yellow bat (*Lasiurus intermedius*), the Seminole bat (*L. seminolus*), and the eastern pipistrelle (*Pipistrellus subflavus*). Florida Scientist. 62: 185-193.

NatureServe. 2002. NatureServe explorer: an online encyclopedia of life [Web application]. Version 4.1. http://www.natureserve.org.

Rafinesque, C.S. 1818. Further discoveries in natural history, made during a journey through the Western States. American Monthly Magazine. 3: 445-446.

Reidinger, R.F., Jr. 1976. Organochlorine residues in adults of six southwestern bat species. Journal of Wildlife Management. 40: 677-680.

Reidinger, R.F., Jr.; Cockrum, E.L. 1978. Organochlorine residues in free-tailed bats (*Tadarida brasiliensis*) at Eagle Creek Cave, Greenlee County, Arizona. In: Proceedings, Fourth International Bat Research Conference. Nairobi, Kenya: Kenya Literature Bureau: 85-96.

Sparks, D.W.; Laborda, J.A.; Whitaker, J.O., Jr. 1998. Bats of the Indianapolis international airport as compared to a more rural community of bats at Prairie Creek. In: Proceedings, Indiana Academy of Science. 107: 171-179.

Speakman, J.; Racey, P.A.; Webb, P.I.; Catto, C.M.C.; Swift, S.M.; Burnett, A.M. 1991. Minimum summer populations and densities of bats in N.E. Scotland, near the northern borders of their distributions. Journal of Zoology London. 225: 327-345.

Tuttle, M.D. 1979. Status, causes of decline, and management of endangered gray bats. Journal of Wildlife Management. 43: 1-17.

U.S. Department of Agriculture. 2003. Forest Inventory and Analysis. U.S. Department of Agriculture, Forest Service.

Watkins, L.C. 1970. Observations on the distribution and natural history of the evening bat (*Nycticeius humeralis*) in northwestern Missouri and adjacent Iowa. Kansas Academy of Science. 72(3): 330-336.

Watkins, L.C. 1972. *Nycticeius humeralis*. Mammalian Species. 23.

Watkins, L.C.; Shump, K.A., Jr. 1981. Behavior of the evening bat *Nycticeius humeralis* at a nursery roost. American Midland Naturalist. 105(2): 260-268.

Whitaker, J.O. 1972. Food habits of bats from Indiana. Canadian Journal of Zoology. 50: 877-883.

Whitaker, J.O.; Brack, J.V.; Cope, J.B. 2002. Are bats in Indiana declining? In: Proceedings, Indiana Academy of Science. 111: 95-106.

Whitaker, J.O.; Clem, P. 1992. Food of the evening bat *Nycticeius humeralis* from Indiana. American Midland Naturalist. 127(1): 211-214.

Whitaker, J.O.; Clem, P.; Munsee, J.R. 1991. Trophic structure of the community in the guano of evening bat *Nycticeius humeralis* in Indiana. American Midland Naturalist. 126: 392-398.

Whitaker, J.O.; Gummer, S.L. 1988. Bat colonies in Indiana, with emphasis on the evening bat, *Nycticeius humeralis*. In: Proceedings, Indiana Academy of Science. 98: 595-598.

Whitaker, J.O.; Gummer, S.L. 1993. The status of the evening bat, *Nyciceius humeralis*, in Indiana. In: Proceedings, Indiana Academy of Science. 102: 283-291.

Whitaker, J.O.; Gummer, S.L. 2001. Bats of the Wabash and Ohio River Basins of southwestern Indiana. In: Proceedings, Indiana Academy of Science. 110: 126-140.

Whitaker, J.O.; Gummer, S.L. 2003. Current status of the evening bat, *Nycticeius humeralis*. In: Proceedings, Indiana Academy of Science. 112(1): 55-60.

Whitaker, J.O., Jr.; Weeks, H.P., Jr. 2001. Food of *Eptesicus fuscus*, the big brown bat, in Indiana in the absence of cultivated fields and agricultural pests. In: Proceedings, Indiana Academy of Science. 110: 123-125.

Wilkinson, G.S. 1992. Information transfer at evening at colonies. Animal Behavior. 44(3): 501-518.

Conservation Assessment: *Myotis austroriparius* (Southeastern Myotis) in the Eastern United States

Sybill Amelon[1], Mark Yates[2], and Craig Pullins[2]

Taxonomy and Nomenclature

The southeastern myotis [*Myotis austroriparius* (Rhoads 1897) (f. G. *mys* mouse; *otis* ear; and L. *austro* southern; *riparius* edges of streams—i.e., southern mouse-eared bat using edges of streams)] belongs to the class Mammalia, order Chiroptera, family Vespertilionidae, subfamily Vespertilioninae, genus/ species *Myotis austroriparius* (LaVal 1970). Type location is Tarpon Springs, Pinellas County, Florida. *M. austroriparius* is considered monotypic (LaVal 1970). *M. a. gatesi* (Lowery 1943) and *M. a. mumfordi* (Rice 1957) are synonyms. Mississippi myotis is an alternative common name.

Description of Species

M. austroriparius (southeastern myotis) is a medium-size member of the genus *Myotis*. Characteristic measurements of the *M. austroriparius* include forearm length, 31 to 41 millimeters (mm) (Jones and Manning 1989, Choate et al. 1994); total length, 77 to 97 mm; tail length, 26 to 44 mm; hindfoot length, 7 to 11 mm (*M. austroriparius'* mean foot length of 10.7 is usually larger than that of similar-sized *Myotis* species); ear length, 11 to 16 mm; skull, usually less than 15 mm. Weight ranges from 5.1 to 8.1 grams (g) (Jones and Manning 1989, Choate et al. 1994). On average, females are slightly larger than males. This species has short, thick, woolly fur that dorsally ranges from russet or bright orange-brown to dark gray, and ventrally ranges from tan to white. Hairs at the venter often have whitish tips (Humphrey and Gore 1992, LaVal 1970, Gardner et al. 1992). The southeastern myotis molts in late summer, shedding a lighter, rusty coat to acquire one of dark gray. Fur may be bi-colored, russet, dark gray, or black at the base, and whitish at the tips. Newly molted pelage has little contrast between the base and tips of hair (Barbour

and Davis 1969, Hall 1981). The hairs on the toes extend past the ends of the claws. The calcar is not keeled. The tragus of the *M. austroriparius* is relatively short and blunt compared to other *Myotis*. The skull is high and domed with a sagital crest and has an abruptly rising forehead. The dental formula is i 2/3, c 1/1, p 3/3, m 3/3, total 38 (Jones and Manning 1989).

M. austroriparius is similar to the Indiana bat (*M. sodalis*), gray bat (*M. grisescens*), and little brown bat (*M. lucifugus*). The Indiana bat lacks long hairs on the toes and has a slightly to moderately keeled calcar. The gray bat is larger than the southeastern myotis; it has uni-colored fur and lacks contrasting whitish tips on its venter, and its wing membrane attaches at the ankle instead of the base of the toes. The little brown bat also lacks contrasting whitish tips on its venter and is slightly smaller then the southeastern myotis.

Biology, Life History, and Natural History

Reproductive Biology and Phenology

The few details available on *M. austroriparius* reproduction were gathered mostly from studies in Florida. A prominent characteristic of reproduction among northern cave-dwelling species is delayed fertilization—an adaptation for minimizing energetically expensive mating activities when energy reserves are lowest after hibernation. Copulation occurs in autumn; the female stores sperm during the winter and ovulates when she emerges from hibernation (Humphrey 1982). In contrast to the norm for most eastern bats, *M. austroriparius* is polygamous, breeding in the spring in southern populations and possibly in the fall or spring in northern populations. In Florida, *M. austroriparius* begins forming maternity colonies in late March (Rice 1957). Female *M. austroriparius* bats gather in large maternity colonies with mean densities of 150 bats per square foot. Males and nonbreeding females generally roost in locations other than the maternity colony. Rice (1957)

---

[1] Wildlife biologist, U.S. Department of Agriculture, Forest Service, North Central Research Station, Columbia, MO.

[2] Graduate assistants, Department of Fisheries and Wildlife Science, University of Missouri, Columbia, MO.

found maternity colonies were associated with standing water in caves. Roosting over water is thought to reduce predation during roosting and to provide increased humidity at roosting sites (Jones and Manning 1989, Foster et al. 1978). In more recent surveys, however, Gore and Hovis (1998) did not find a significant association between roosting and the presence of water in a cave.

Parturition occurs in mid-April to early May in Florida (Rice 1957) and in May in Illinois (Gardner et al. 1992). In contrast to other species of *Myotis* species, which have one offspring per litter, southeastern myotis commonly have two offspring per litter (mean = litter size is 1.9) (Hermanson and Wilkins 1986, Rice 1957, Foster et al. 1978). This higher fecundity rate has been hypothesized to be an adaptation to increased exposure to in-flight predation because of longer periods of annual activity (Foster et al. 1978). Sherman (1930) reported the birth weights of two *M. austroriparius* bats at 1.10 and 1.15 g from a female weighing 7.25 g. These fetal weights represent approximately 31 percent of the maternal weight, which is similar to single fetal weights reported for other *Myotis* species. Foster et al. (1978) found that all deciduous teeth were present at birth. Young are born hairless and pink with eyes closed and pinnae folded (Sherman 1930). The habit of roosting over water may increase the fatality of nonvolant juveniles that fall to the roost floor (Rice 1957). Parturition synchrony, combined with clustering in maternity colonies, should increase metabolic rates and lead to rapid postnatal growth rates (Stevenson and Tuttle 1982). At birth, the sex ratio is at parity (Hermanson and Wilkins 1986, Rice 1957), but Rice (1957) found a shift in this ratio among adults. A decrease in the number of adult males found in hibernacula was attributed to males using less-protected roosting sites during spring and summer while females were in maternity colonies.

Young are left in clusters in the maternity colony while the adults leave to forage. Young become volant at 5 to 6 weeks after birth. Rice (1957) captured flying juveniles as early as June 9 in Florida. In Texas, Horner et al. (1998) found that parturition occurs in late April to early May and that the young become volant by the end of May, several weeks earlier than young in Florida. Juveniles are sexually mature and able to breed the following spring (Rice 1957).

In Florida, male *M. austroriparius* were found to have enlarged epididymides from mid-February to mid-April (Rice 1957). Gardner et al. (1992) found that males captured in Illinois followed trends similar to those of Florida populations; scrotal testes were found only in May.

Ecology and Behavior

Winter hibernacula and summer maternity sites are generally in different locations (Mumford and Whitaker 1982, Rice 1957). Migration routes are not documented, but Rice (1957) recorded movement distances of 28.9 to 72.4 kilometers (km) for banded individuals. Dispersal from maternity colonies begins in October, with males leaving earlier than females. Rice (1957) found the number of individuals at Florida maternity colonies declined markedly by the end of October; all individuals were gone by the second week of December. The number of individuals found in hibernating sites increases following departure from maternity roots. There does not seem to be any migration of individuals. There is, however, a shift in roost locations between spring and summer sites and overwintering sites (Gardner et al. 1992).

In Florida, maternity colonies form during March and April (Rice 1957). During the maternity period, few males are found in maternity colonies. After the young mature, however, males may join the females in maternity colonies (Rice 1957).

Lowery (1974) observed *M. austroriparius* roosting in buildings and hollow trees. In Arkansas, this species has been found using old mines, buildings, hollow trees (Sealander 1979), and bridges. In Illinois, Kentucky, Tennessee, Indiana, and Mississippi, caves are the most frequently used roosting sites (Barbour and Davis 1969, Mumford and Whitaker 1982). In Arkansas, Heath et al. (1986) reported hibernating colonies in abandoned mines. Graves and Harvey (1974) reported *M. austroriparius* as the second most commonly captured bat over ponds and streams in western Tennessee.

Obligate associations with other species have not been observed. *M. austroriparius* has been found in maternity colonies in Florida with gray bats (Wenner 1984) and free-tailed bats (Hermanson and Wilkins 1986, Sherman 1930). *M. austroriparius* also shares bachelor roosts and winter roosts with other species, including free-tailed bats (*Tadarida brasilensis*), eastern pipistrelles (*Pipistrellus subflavus*), big brown bats (*Eptesicus fuscus*), and evening bats (*Nycticeius humeralis*) (Bain 1981, Gore and Hovis 1994, Rice 1957).

Hibernation

Mammalian hibernation is characterized by periods of torpor interrupted cyclically by spontaneous arousal. Individuals aroused during hibernation tend to fly or move around between periods of torpor. Unlike many species of *Myotis*, *M. austroriparius* has a variable hibernation strategy. This strategy is possibly an adaptation to survival in a warmer climate. In the northern parts of its range, *M. austroriparius* may hibernate from September or October until February or March. In southern areas, this species remains active throughout much of the winter (Jones and Manning 1989). Males and females roost together in hibernacula (Humphrey and Gore 1992). During hibernation, southeastern myotis bats usually roost in clusters of up to 50 individuals in caves or buildings (Jones and Pagels 1968, Lowery 1974, Mumford and Whitaker 1982). The species may also use mines or bridges (Wilhide 2001, Saugey et al. 1989). In some portions of its range, *M. austroriparius* may hibernate in association with *M. lucifugus* (Mumford and Whitaker 1982), *T. brasiliensis* (Sherman 1930, 1939), *P. subflavus* and *Corynorhinus rafinesquii* (Jones and Suttkus 1973, 1975; Mirowsky and Horner 1997), and *E. fuscus* (Best et al. 1992, Saugey et al. 1993, Walker et al. 1996).

Food Habits

M. austroriparius is associated with water. It forages low over the water's surface, feeding on a variety of insect taxa (Rice 1955, Zinn and Humphrey 1981). This species leaves the roost after dusk to forage (Gardner et al. 1992). On warmer nights in early spring and summer, Zinn and Humphrey (1981) studied *M. austroriparius* in Florida and found it to be a generalist that shows a preference for dipterans, coleopterans, and lepidopterans later in the season. Some have suggested that selectivity for dipterans was an adaptation to the longer period of activity and reproduction. Schmidly et al. (1977) reported southeastern myotis foraging over slow-moving streams adjacent to upland areas with loblolly (*Pinus taeda*) and shortleaf (*P. echinata*) pine with mixed hardwoods. Other reported foraging types include mature, forested wetlands in Illinois (Gardner et al. 1992) and Texas (Horner 1995); forested

streams in Tennessee (Graves and Harvey 1974); live oaks and shrubby old fields in Florida (Zinn and Humphrey 1981), and bottom-land hardwood and in baldcypress (*Taxodium distichum*)–tupelo gum (*Nyssa aquatica*) swamp in Arkansas and South Carolina (Clark et al. 1998, Hoffman et al. 1998).

Mortality and Predation Factors

Limited research has been conducted to determine the mortality and survivorship of *M. austroriparius*. Again, the available information is related to Florida populations. Rice (1957) estimated the annual survival rate is 46 percent for a stable population. He determined this estimate by calculating the rate of mortality for the population at a stable level when the birth rate is 116 percent. Therefore, this estimate may not hold true for declining populations. Because of the species' colonial behavior in caves and other structures associated with water, flooding or other disturbances pose a relatively high potential for catastrophic losses. Foster et al. (1978) reported preweaning mortality to be fairly high—about 12 percent for colonies roosting over water. Rice (1957) hypothesized that the presence of water beneath maternity colonies increased preweaning mortality rates due to dislodged juveniles drowning.

Predation by rat snakes (*Elaphe spp.*), raccoons (*Procyon lotor*), and owls (*Bubo spp.* and *Strix spp.*) has been observed but not in large enough numbers to cause decline concerns. Various helminthes inhabit the digestive tracts of *M. austroriparius,* but its parasite community is small compared to other *Myotis* species from the Midwest (Lotz and Font 1991). Rice (1957) and Mumford and Whitaker (1982) reported that mites, parasitic flies, chiggers, and intestinal trematodes use *M. austroriparius* as a host species.

Longevity

There were no estimates on longevity.

Banding Data

Banding efforts by Allen (1921) marked initial attempts to study migration in North American bats. Rice (1957) documented a single banded individual recovered 43.2 km from the roost site. The mean distance traveled by 14 banded individuals was 17 km estimated by recaptures.

Site Fidelity

Fidelity to maternity roost sites is thought to be relatively high among *M. austroriparius* (Gore and Hovis 1998, Rice 1957) based on very few records. Mumford and Whitaker (1975) recaptured several bats banded in the previous year, which may indicate roost-site fidelity from year to year.

Distribution

M. austroriparius has a disjunct distribution (Hamilton and Whitaker 1979) (fig. 1). Miller and Allen (1928) described three subspecies based on geographic locations and pelage color. LaVal (1970) examined the morphological and pelage characteristics and determined no distinct character would allow differentiation. Life history characteristics may differ, however, among the three distinct geographic populations, primarily due to climatic characteristics that allow the southernmost populations to remain active all year while the northern populations hibernate. *M. austroriparius* is most common in Florida where it is well adapted to the climate. Surveys have not been conducted to estimate the total population of *M. austroriparius*.

Figure 1. *The distribution of* Myotis austroriparius.

* = Isolated or questionable records.

Source: Bat Conservation International 2003, http://www.batcon.org.

M. austroriparius lives in the Southeastern United States from coastal southeastern Virginia and eastern North Carolina, south into peninsular Florida, west through Louisiana and into eastern Texas, northward through southeastern Arkansas, and into the Mississippi River Valley to southern Illinois and Indiana. The species also is believed to live in certain areas along the lower Ohio River Valley in Kentucky, Indiana, and Illinois. Barbour and Davis (1969) suggested declining numbers in Illinois, Indiana, and Kentucky and concluded the species was nearing extinction in the Ohio River Valley. Gardner et al. (1992) found *M. austroriparius* in only one of nine previously reported winter roosts in Illinois and concluded, based on consensus of more than 40 authorities from States within this bat's range, that the population is in serious decline and should receive at least a federally threatened status.

Habitat Requirements

Maternity Period (May to August)

Roosting Habitat

Maternity roosts are thought to be the most important component of summer habitat because young are born and reared on these sites (Gore and Hovis 1994, Humphrey and Gore 1992, Rice 1957). Southern populations (specifically those in peninsular Florida) typically form maternity colonies in warm caves. Rice (1957) believed that maternity caves in Florida required permanent water with a large area of horizontal ceiling above the water. These conditions are believed to maintain high humidity and stable temperatures at the roost and provide protection from predators (Rice 1955, Tuttle 1975, Zinn 1977). More recently, however, surveys of Florida maternity caves found only two of eight caves with pools under the roosts; four caves were completely dry under the roosts (Gore and Hovis 1994).

The physical characteristics that make a cave suitable as a maternity roost are not well understood. Zinn (1977) suggested that caves with domed ceilings trapped metabolic heat and provided a stable temperature regime while outside temperatures fluctuated during the nursery period. Recent studies have suggested that human disturbance rather than cave structure may be the factor determining maternity cave use.

In other regions of the species' range, maternity colonies use alternative structures. In east Texas, maternity colonies were located in hollow trees of bottom-land hardwood forests (Horner and Mirowski 1996, Mirowsky 1997). Schmidly et al. (1977) found *M. austroriparius* in oak- and longleaf pine (*Pinus palustris*) forest types. *M. austroriparius* has been captured in baldcypress–tupelo gum swamps in North Carolina (Clark et al. 1985) and Illinois (Gardner et al. 1992). Roost trees were typically in large, live black and tupelo gum trees with triangular entrances near their bases. The cavities extended 3 to 8 meters (m) up the tree and the colony was located near the top; these trees were typically surrounded by water. *M. austroriparius* in Tennessee (Graves and Harvey 1974) and Kentucky (Gardner et al. 1992) were captured in mature floodplain forests.

Maternity colonies of *M. austroriparius* have been reported in chimneys (Foster et al. 1978), concrete culverts (Bain 1981), buildings (Lowery 1974, Kern et al. 1996), mine shafts (Sealander 1979), and bridges (Wilhide 2001). Typically, few males are found in maternity colonies. Males are believed to roost alone or in small bachelor colonies during the summer. The specific roost types are not well documented (Hamilton and Whitaker 1979).

Movement between summer and winter habitats is usually local, barely qualifying as migration. Most individuals leave maternity sites in late September or October and gather in protected roost sites, frequently over water, to spend the winter.

Foraging Habitat

There is a dearth of published information on foraging habitat for this species. As mentioned earlier, Rice (1957) documented a single banded individual recovered 43.2 km from the roost site. The mean distance traveled by 14 banded, recaptured individuals was 17 km. Gardner et al. (1992) tracked radio-tagged individuals foraging up to 2 km from roosting sites. These differences in distance traveled seem to indicate that, as with many aspects of this species, the southern and northern populations may behave differently.

M. austroriparius bats leave their roosts somewhat later than other bats and fly to ponds, swamps, rivers, or lakes (Barbour and Davis 1969). They fly low over the water, capturing small moths, beetles, midges, and mosquitoes (Zinn

and Humphrey 1981). Foraging activities center around habitats associated with water, including streams, rivers, lakes, ponds, swamps, forested wetlands, and bottom-land hardwoods.

Hibernation Period (October to April)

Throughout most of its range, *M. austroriparius* is predominantly a cave bat (Gore and Hovis 1998, Rice 1957). In Louisiana, however, it is thought to use hollow trees and buildings exclusively because of the lack of caves (Lowery 1974, Rice 1957). In Arkansas, this species has been found hibernating in mines and hand-dug wells (Davis et al. 1955, Heath et al. 1986, Saugey et al. 1993). It has also been found using human-made structures, bridges, culverts (Gardner et al. 1992, Gore 2002), and barns (Bain 1981) for winter roosts.

In winter, this species hibernates in caves for shorter periods than many other species do. In contrast to other *Myotis* species, *M. austroriparius* do not appear to be obligatory hibernators. It puts on little or no fat, uses torpor only during short cold spells, and remains active during the winter, which may be an adaptation to the more continuous food supply available in warmer climates (McNab 1974). Peninsular Florida populations were found to be active throughout the year, foraging during warm periods. These populations may become dormant during periods of colder weather, but they do not truly hibernate as do more northern populations (Rice 1957). Peninsular Florida populations do, however, move from summer roosts to winter roosts. In the panhandle of Florida and adjacent areas, bats were found to enter torpor for short periods, leaving to forage during warmer periods. Humphrey and Gore (1992) reported activity of thousands of *M. austroriparius* at two maternity caves from December through March, indicating these bats are active all winter in more southerly locations.

In more northerly geographic locations, southeastern myotis do hibernate, often in caves or mines. Gardner et al. (1992) found that in the upper Mississippi and Ohio River regions, this species is in hibernacula from late September to March. Often, even in the colder areas of this species' range, bats were found to be awake or easily disturbed during the hibernation period, suggesting an adaptation toward shallow torpor rather than true hibernation. Where average winter temperatures are warmer, this type of behavior may allow for more opportunistic feeding during warmer periods or mild winters. A colony of *M. austroriparius* was discovered in an abandoned cotton mill north of Raleigh, NC (Webster et al. 1984). The number of bats in this colony fluctuated, with highest numbers present from April to December; few individuals remained from January to March. These bats were observed going into torpor when ambient temperatures dropped to 5 °C. Harvey et al. (1991) reported colonies of up to 3,000 bats in western Kentucky caves.

Potential Threats

Natural or Human Factors

Disturbance during hibernation or maternity periods is a significant factor in the widespread decline of cave- and mine-dependent bat species (Clark et al. 1998, Currie 1999). The foremost factor leading to population declines is destruction of roost sites, particularly hibernacula (Humphrey 1975, Sheffield and Chapman 1992). Rice (1955) found 11,000 *M. austroriparius* bats in Mud Cave, which has since become a dumping site (Humphrey and Gore 1992). The entrances of two additional Florida caves have been blocked (Gore and Hovis 1994), one with wire fencing to reduce trespassing and the other with rock removed from a nearby agricultural site. Guano piles set on fire resulted in the abandonment of another maternity cave in Florida (Gore and Hovis 1994). In Alabama, a large maternity colony was reported extirpated because of vandals and careless cave explorers (Mount 1986).

Human disturbance also includes indirect habitat disturbance. Noise and lights from cave exploration occurring during hibernation may awaken or disturb roosting bats and cause them to abandon the caves and result in depleting their fat supplies. In maternity colonies, disturbance may induce adults to fly, resulting in young being knocked from the roost leading to juvenile mortality (Foster et al. 1978, Hermanson and Wilkins 1986).

Natural environmental events, such as flooding of caves or roost trees, exacerbated by land use changes, may seriously impact *M. austroriparius* populations. About 57,000 bats were killed in a flood at Snead's Cave in Florida in 1990 (Gore and Hovis 1994). Increased frequency of flooding by

impoundments or channelization in areas used by bats may increase mortality rates.

Blocking or plugging cave entrances changes airflow patterns and may change temperature and humidity regimes and subsequently reduce suitable maternity or hibernating habitat (Tuttle 1981). The collapse or destruction of natural or artificial roosting structures such as caves, mines, buildings, or culverts may trap bats or close a roost to future use (Gore and Hovis 1994).

Pesticides used to control insects or chemicals from agricultural runoff may harm bat populations either directly by killing the bats or indirectly by impairing reproductive capability or foraging success. Food chain poisoning by pesticides—in particular, insecticides such as organochlorines and anticholinesterase—has been demonstrated to negatively impact insectivorous bats (Clark 1988a, 1988b, 2001; Clark and Krynitsky 1983; Cockrum 1970; Reidinger and Cockrum 1978; Clark et al. 1983).

Present or Potential Risks to Habitat

Converting or harvesting mature wetland and bottom-land forests may impact *M. austroriparius* in areas where the species roosts in hollow trees or forages in mature wetland and bottom-land forests. Gardner et al. (1992) found *M. austroriparius* foraging in mature forested wetland, much of which has been converted to agriculture within the range of this species. Direct habitat loss of bottom-land hardwood, tupelo gum swamps, cypress swamps, and other forested wetlands has also contributed to the decline of the southeastern myotis (Mirowsky and Horner 1997). Reservoir construction and floodplain protection may impact suitable habitat and roosting sites for this species.

Inadequacy of Existing Regulatory Mechanisms

Early bat roost protection efforts focused on eliminating or reducing disturbances by installing informative signs or "bat friendly" gates and fences to control human disturbance during critical hibernation and maternity periods. In some cases, these efforts were unfavorable because of limited understanding of bat behavior and cave microclimate factors. Some early gate designs altered the air flow patterns of the cave environment, resulting in increased temperatures that were less desirable for hibernation (Currie 1999, Tuttle and Taylor 1995).

Protecting natural and human-made roosting structures is one of the highest priorities in all the recovery plans for listed species (Harvey 1976, USFWS 1983). Funding and access to facilitate these protection measures are often unavailable.

Population Status

Rangewide

Global Heritage Status is G3, G4 and National Heritage Status is N3, N4—indicating *M. austroriparius* may be rare to common. The wide range of status ranking is likely the result of lack of information on this species globally and nationally (NatureServe 2002). Individual State Heritage Status is described in State Summaries and in table 1.

Federal

M. austroriparius was a candidate species (C2) to be listed by the U.S. Fish & Wildlife Service (USFWS) as either threatened or endangered (USFWS 1989). The USFWS, however, discontinued the designation of C2 species as candidates for listing (USFWS 1996). *M. austroriparius* is currently considered a species of concern until more biological research can resolve its conservation status (NatureServe 2002).

State

M. austroriparius is listed as endangered in Illinois, Indiana, Kentucky, and Oklahoma. It is a species of concern in Alabama, Arkansas, Missouri, South Carolina, Texas, and Virginia (table 1).

M. austroriparius is most common in Florida, where it is well adapted to the climate. Surveys have not been conducted to estimate the total population of *M. austroriparius*. Population data are fairly scarce and concerns about accuracy of count methods among areas and sampling methods are cited. Systematic, uniform population surveys have not been routinely conducted in portions of the species' range outside of Florida. Even in Florida, where the best data are available, the population appears to have declined by 16 to 45 percent between 1957 (Rice 1957) and 1994 (Gore and Hovis 1994). Gore and Hovis (1994) compared historical counts from maternity caves from various sources ranging from 1936 to 1982 with counts made in 1991 and 1992. Nine caves with a historical combined maximum use of 140,000 *M. austroriparius* had no individuals in the recent surveys. But recent surveys show that 85,000 individuals occupied four caves lacking historical data.

Demographic information on reproductive rates, recruitment rates, sex ratios, and movements between roosting sites and between maternity roosts and hibernacula in noncave maternity sites would be necessary to quantitatively estimate population viability.

Table 1. *Population status of* Myotis austroriparius *by State.*[1]

State	Status[2]	Historic estimate	Current estimate	Summer habitat (reported)	Winter habitat (reported)	Threats
Alabama	S2	Unknown	3,240[a]	Caves, mines, buildings, and trees	Caves	Human disturbance, loss of suitable roosting sites, loss of habitat
Arkansas	S2	Unknown		Trees and bridges	Caves and mines	Human disturbance, loss of suitable roosting sites, loss of habitat
Florida	S3	400,000[b]	320,000[c]	Caves and buildings	Caves	Human disturbance, loss of suitable roosting sites, loss of habitat
Georgia	S3	Unknown	Few thousand			Human disturbance, loss of suitable roosting sites, loss of habitat

Table 1. *Population status of* Myotis austroriparius *by State[1] (continued).*

State	Status[2]	Historic estimate	Current estimate	Summer habitat (reported)	Winter habitat (reported)	Threats
Illinois	**S1**	**Unknown**	**Unknown**	**Trees**	**Caves and mines**	**Human disturbance, loss of suitable roosting sites, loss of habitat**
Indiana	**S1**	**Unknown**	**Presumed extirpated**	**NA**	**NA**	**Human disturbance, loss of suitable roosting sites, loss of habitat**
Kentucky	S1	Unknown	Unknown		Trees, caves, mines, and bridges	Human disturbance, loss of suitable roosting sites, loss of habitat
Louisiana	S4	Unknown		Trees	Trees	Human disturbance, loss of suitable roosting sites, loss of habitat
Mississippi	S1	Unknown				Human disturbance, loss of suitable roosting sites, loss of habitat
Missouri	**SU**	**Unknown**	**Unknown**		**Unknown**	**Human disturbance, loss of suitable roosting sites, loss of habitat**
North Carolina		Unknown		Trees		Human disturbance, loss of suitable roosting sites, loss of habitat
Oklahoma	S1	Unknown		Trees		Human disturbance, loss of suitable roosting sites, loss of habitat
South Carolina	S2, S3	Unknown		Trees		Human disturbance, loss of suitable roosting sites, loss of habitat
Tennessee	S3	Unknown				Human disturbance, loss of suitable roosting sites, loss of habitat
Texas	S3	Unknown		Trees	Buildings, bridges, and caves	Human disturbance, loss of suitable roosting sites, loss of habitat
Virginia	S1, S2	Unknown				Human disturbance, loss of suitable roosting sites, loss of habitat

[a] Hudson, 1999.

[b] Rice, 1957.

[c] Gore and Hovis, 1998.

[1] Information about population and habitat use is based on literature cited. See text and References section.

[2] Status based on Natural Heritage State Rarity ranks (NatureServe 2002). S1: Extremely rare; usually five or fewer occurrences in the State, or, in the case of communities, covering less than 50 hectares (ha) in aggregate; or may have a few remaining individuals; often especially vulnerable to extirpation. S2: Very rare; usually between 5 and 20 occurrences, or, in the case of communities, covering less than 250 ha in aggregate; or few occurrences with many individuals; often susceptible to becoming endangered. S3: Rare to uncommon; usually between 20 and 100 occurrences; may have fewer occurrences, but with a large number of individuals in some populations; may be susceptible to large-scale disturbances. S4: Common; usually more than 100 occurrences, but may be fewer with many large populations; may be restricted to only a portion of the State; usually not susceptible to immediate threats. SNR/SU: Status not ranked/Status uncertain, often because of low search effort or cryptic nature of the element. States in **BOLD** occur in Region 9.

Habitat Status

Summary of Land Ownership and Existing Habitat Protection

National Forests

Estimates of the potential available habitat for *M. austrori-parius* were based on U.S. Department of Agriculture (USDA) Forest Service Forest Inventory and Analysis (FIA) data, which estimate the amount of upland hardwood and pine-hardwood forest land more than 60 years old for all States with national forests in Regions 8 and 9 (Southern and Eastern Forest Service Regions combined to look at the entire species range) and Region 9 (examined alone to look at potential available habitat for States in the Eastern Region), excluding rarely used decidu-ous forest types such as aspen. This coarse-scale assessment of habitat availability considers forest type and age class based on USDA Forest Service FIA data (USDA Forest Service 2003). This analysis does not consider other aspects of forest structure that may influence use by this species. The database used is subject to sampling errors associated with coarse-scale inventory. Estimates were for the acreage of upland hardwood and pine-hardwood forest land for forests of all ownerships,

including other federally owned, State-owned, county/munici-pal-owned, and privately owned lands within these States. Ap-proximately 3.8 percent of upland hardwood, bottom-land hard-wood, and pine-hardwood forest types occur on National Forest System (NFS) lands within the range of this species; less than 1 percent occur on NFS lands within Region 9. Ninety percent of the potential habitat for this species occurs on privately owned lands (figs. 2 and 5). Estimates indicate that 347,529,086 acres of upland hardwood, bottom-land hardwood, and pine-hard-wood forest land that could potentially serve as foraging habitat occur within the range of this species. Estimates also indicate that stands more than 60 years old in upland hardwood, bottom-land hardwood, and pine-hardwood forest types would provide suitable trees to meet the roosting requirements of this species. Within the range of *M. austroriparius*, estimates indicate that 93,673,155 acres, or 27 percent of the total available, are more than 60 years old (figs. 3 and 4). On NFS lands within Region 9, estimates indicate that 11,359,361 acres of potential habitat (upland hardwood, bottom-land hardwood, and pine-hardwood forest types) and 3,925,418 acres of upland hardwood and pine-hardwood forest types more than 60 years old (34.5 percent) are available for roosting and foraging (figs. 3 and 4).

Figure 2. *Ownership of upland hardwood, bottom-land hardwood, and pine-hardwood forest types within States overlapping the range of* M. austroriparius.

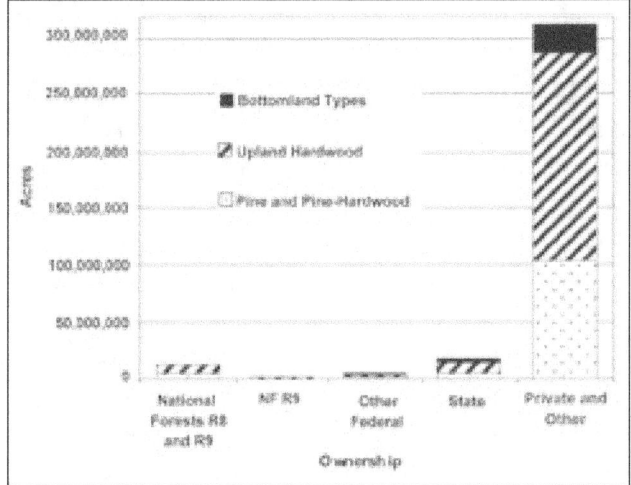

Alabama, Arkansas, Florida, Georgia, Illinois, Indiana, Kentucky, Louisiana, Mississippi, Missouri, North Carolina, Oklahoma, South Carolina, Tennessee, Texas, Virginia.

Figure 3. *Acreage by ownership of upland hardwood forest type and percentage of upland hardwood forest type more than 60 years old by ownership within States overlapping the range of* M. austroriparius.

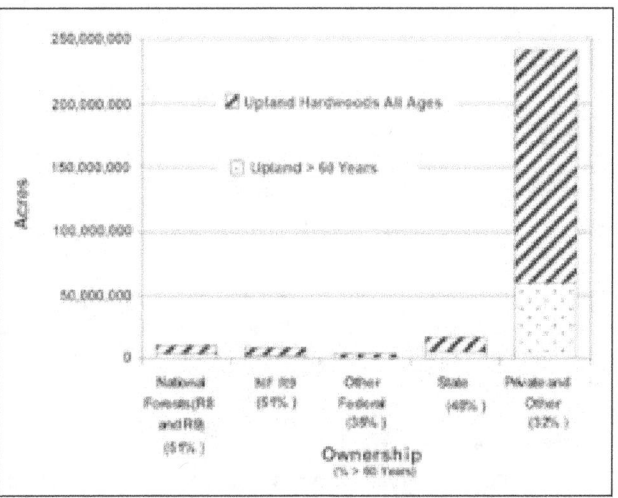

Alabama, Arkansas, Florida, Georgia, Illinois, Indiana, Kentucky, Louisiana, Mississippi, Missouri, North Carolina, Oklahoma, South Carolina, Tennessee, Texas, Virginia.

Figure 4. *Acreage by ownership of pine and pine-hardwood forest types and percentage of pine and pine-hardwood forest types more than 60 years old by ownership within States overlapping the range of* M. austroriparius.

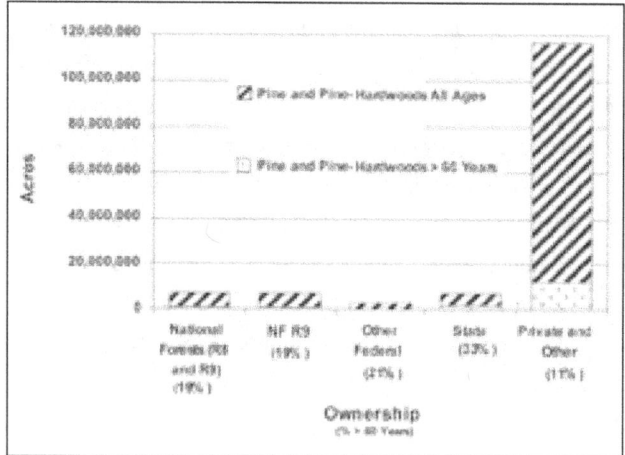

Alabama, Arkansas, Florida, Georgia, Illinois, Indiana, Kentucky, Louisiana, Mississippi, Missouri, North Carolina, Oklahoma, South Carolina, Tennessee, Texas, Virginia.

Figure 5. *Acreage by ownership of bottom-land hardwood forest type and percentage of bottom-land hardwood forest type more than 60 years old by ownership within States overlapping the range of* M. austroriparius.

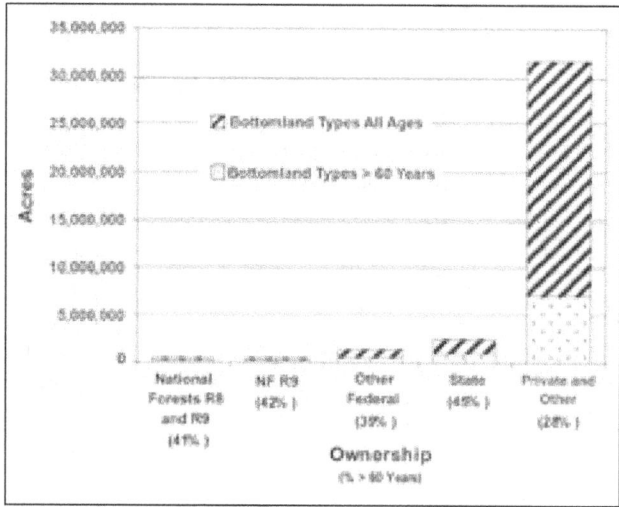

Alabama, Arkansas, Florida, Georgia, Illinois, Indiana, Kentucky, Louisiana, Mississippi, Missouri, North Carolina, Oklahoma, South Carolina, Tennessee, Texas, Virginia.

State Summaries

Only three States in Region 9 are within the range of *M. austroriparius*. Missouri has a few individuals, as evidenced by

captures in the Bootheel Region in 2000 to 2002; none have been captured on the Mark Twain National Forest during fairly extensive surveys (Aars and Ims 2000, Amelon 2001). Mist-net surveys have been conducted in areas of potential habitat in several States. In South Carolina, Texas, and Illinois, surveys of old growth, bottomland, and swamp forests have been conducted (Clark et al. 1985, Gardner et al. 1991, Horner 1995, Horner and Mirowski 1996, Mirowsky et al. 2004). The primary objective of these surveys was to determine presence and distribution of the species rather than population size. This species is believed extirpated from Indiana (Whitaker et al. 2002).

References

Aars, J.; Ims, R.A. 2000. Population dynamic and genetic consequences of spatial density-dependent dispersal in patchy populations. The American Naturalist. 155(2): 252-265.

Allen, A.A. 1921. Banding bats. Journal of Mammalogy. 2: 53-57.

Amelon, S.K. 2001. Unpublished data. Columbia, MO: U.S. Department of Agriculture, Forest Service, North Central Research Station.

Bain, J.R. 1981. Roosting ecology of three Florida bats: *Nycticeius humeralis, Myotis austroriparius, Tadarida brasiliensis*. Gainesville, FL: University of Florida. 88 p. M.S. thesis.

Barbour, R.W.; Davis, W.H. 1969. Bats of America. Lexington, KY: University of Kentucky Press. 286 p.

Best, T.L.; Carey, S.D.; Henry, T.H.; Caesar, K.G. 1992. Distribution and abundance of bats (Mammalia: Chiroptera) in coastal plain caves of southern Alabama. NSS Bulletin. 225: 61-65.

Choate, J.R.; Jones, J.K.; Jones, J.C. 1994. Handbook of mammals of the South-Central States. Baton Rouge, LA: Louisiana State University Press. 336 p.

Clark, D.R.; Bunck, C.M.; Cromartie, E.; LaVal, R.K. 1983. Year and age effects on residues of dieldrin and heptachlor in dead gray bats, Franklin County, Missouri—1976, 1977, and 1978. Environmental Toxicology and Chemistry. 2: 387-393.

Clark, D.R., Jr. 1988a. Environmental contaminants and the management of bat populations in the United States. In: Proceedings, symposium on management of amphibians, reptiles, and small mammals in North America. Laurel, MD: U.S. Fish & Wildlife Service: 409-413.

Clark, D.R., Jr. 1988b. How sensitive are bats to insecticides? Wildlife Society Bulletin. 16: 399-403.

Clark, D.R., Jr. 2001. DDT and the decline of free-tailed bats (*Tadarida brasiliensis*) at Carlsbad Caverns, New Mexico. Archives of Environmental Contamination and Toxicology. 40: 537-543.

Clark, D.R., Jr.; Cantu, R.; Cowman, D.F.; Maxson, D.J. 1998. Uptake of arsenic and metals by tadpoles at an historically contaminated Texas site. Ecotoxicology. 7: 61-67.

Clark, D.R., Jr.; Krynitsky, A.J. 1983. DDE in brown and white fat of hibernating bats. Environmental Toxicology and Chemistry. 31: 287-299.

Clark, M.K.; David, S.L.; Funderburg, J.B., Jr. 1985. The mammal fauna of Carolina bays, pocosins and associated communities in North Carolina: an overview. Brimleyana. 11: 1-38.

Cockrum, E.L. 1970. Insecticides and guano bats. Ecology. 51: 761-762.

Currie, R.R. 1999. An overview of the response of bats to protection efforts. In: Proceedings, Indiana Bat Symposium. Lexington, KY: Bat Conservation International. 24 p.

Davis, W.H.; Lidicker, W.Z., Jr.; Sealander, J.A., Jr. 1955. *Myotis austroriparius* in Arkansas. Journal of Mammalogy. 36: 288.

Foster, G.W.; Humphrey, S.R.; Humphrey, P.P. 1978. Survival rate of young southeastern brown bats, *Myotis austroriparius*, in Florida. Journal of Mammalogy. 59(2): 299-304.

Gardner, J.E.; Garner, J.D.; Hofmann, J.E. 1991. Final report: summer roost selection and roosting behavior of *Myotis sodalis* (Indiana bat) in Illinois. Chicago: Illinois Natural History Survey Division; Illinois Department of Conservation. 51 p.

Gardner, J.E.; Hofman, J.E.; Krejca, J.K.; Garner, J.D.; Robinson, S.E. 1992. Final report: distribution and status of *Myotis austroriparius* (southeastern bat) in Illinois. Springfield, IL: Illinois Department of Conservation. 44 p.

Gore, J.A. 2002. Personal communication. Wildlife biologist, Florida Fish and Wildlife Conservation Commission, Tallahassee, FL. Conversation.

Gore, J.A.; Hovis, J.A. 1994. Southeastern myotis maternity cave survey. Survey report. Florida Game and Fresh Water Fish Commission. 10 p.

Gore, J.A.; Hovis, J.A. 1998. Status and conservation of southeastern myotis maternity colonies in Florida caves. Florida Scientist. 61(3/4): 160-170.

Graves, F.F.; Harvey, M.J. 1974. Distribution of Chiroptera in western Tennessee. Journal of the Tennessee Academy of Science. 49(3): 106-109.

Hall, E.R. 1981. The mammals of North America. New York: John Wiley & Sons. 600 p.

Hamilton, W.J.; Whitaker, J.O., Jr. 1979. Mammals of the Eastern United States. Ithaca, NY: Cornell University Press. 346 p.

Harvey, M.J. 1976. Endangered Chiroptera of the Southeastern United States. Proceedings, Southeastern Association of Game and Fish Commission. 29: 429-433.

Harvey, M.J.; MacGregor, J.R.; Currie, R.R. 1991. Distribution and status of Chiroptera in Kentucky and Tennessee. Journal of the Tennessee Academy of Science. 4: 191-193.

Heath, D.R.; Saugey, D.A.; Heidt, G.A. 1986. Abandoned mine fauna of the Ouachita Mountains, Arkansas: vertebrate taxa. Proceedings, Arkansas Academy of Science. 40: 33-36.

Hermanson, J.W.; Wilkins, K.T. 1986. Pre-weaning mortality in a Florida maternity roost of *Myotis austroriparius* and *Tadarida brasiliensis*. Journal of Mammalogy. 67(4): 754-757.

Hoffman, J.D.; Wilhide, J.D.; Cochran, V.S.; King, S. 1998. Roost tree selection of female *Corynorhinus rafinesquii* and *Myotis austroriparius* in a bottom-land hardwood forest. Bat Research News. 39(4): 170.

Horner, P. 1995. East Texas rare bat survey: final report. Austin, TX: Texas Parks and Wildlife Department, Resources Protection Division. 32 p.

Horner, P.; Mirowski, K. 1996. East Texas rare bat survey: 1995. Final report. Austin, TX: Texas Parks and Wildlife Department, Resources Protection Division. 30 p.

Horner, P.; Mirowski, K.; McDonnell, J.; Clark, M.K. 1998. Status, distribution, and natural history of *Myotis austroriparius* in Texas and the Carolinas. Bat Research News. 39(4): 171.

Humphrey, S.R. 1975. Nursery roosts and community diversity of neararctic bats. Journal of Mammalogy. 56: 321-346.

Humphrey, S.R. 1982. Bats: *Vespertilionidae* and *Molossidae*. In: Chapman, J.A.; Feldhamer, G.A., eds. Wild mammals of North America. Baltimore: John Hopkins University Press: 52-70.

Humphrey, S.R.; Gore, J.A. 1992. Southeastern brown bat. In: Humphrey, S.R., ed. Rare and endangered biota of Florida. Vol. 1. Gainesville, FL: University of Florida: 335-342.

Jones, C.; Manning, R.W. 1989. *Myotis austroriparius*. Mammalian Species. 332: 1-3.

Jones, C.; Pagels, J. 1968. Notes on a population of *Pipistrellus subflavus* in southern Louisiana. Journal of Mammalogy. 49: 134-139.

Jones, C.; Suttkus, R.D. 1973. Colony structure and organization of *Pipistrellus subflavus* in southern Louisiana. Journal of Mammalogy. 54: 962-968.

Jones, C.; Suttkus, R.D. 1975. Notes on the natural history of *Plecotus rafinesquii*. Occas. Pap. 47. New Orleans: Louisiana State University, Museum of Zoology: 38.

Kern, W.H., Jr.; Koehler, P.G.; Belwood, J.J. 1996. Bats in building. Gainesville, FL: University of Florida, Cooperative Extension Services, Institute of Food and Agricultural Science.

LaVal, R.K. 1970. Infraspecific relationships of bats of the species *Myotis austroriparius*. Journal of Mammalogy. 51(3): 542-552.

Lotz, J.A.; Font, W.F. 1991. Determinants of organization and diversity in communities of intestinal helminths of bats. Mississippi Academy of Science Journal. 36(1): 68.

Lowery, G.H., Jr. 1943. Check-list of the mammals of Louisiana and adjacent waters. Occas. Pap. 13. New Orleans: Louisiana State University, Museum of Zoology: 213-257.

Lowery, G.H., Jr. 1974. The mammals of Louisiana and its adjacent waters. Baton Rouge, LA: Louisiana State University Press. 565 p.

McNab, B.K. 1974. The behavior of temperate cave bats in a subtropical environment. Ecology. 55: 943-958.

Miller, G.S.; Allen, G.M. 1928. The American bats of the genera *Myotis* and *Pizonyx*. Bulletin of the United States National Museum. 144: 1-218.

Mirowsky, K.; Horner, P. 1997. Roosting ecology of two rare vespertilionid bats, the southeastern myotis and Rafinesque's big-eared bat, in east Texas. 1996 annual report. Austin, TX: Texas Parks and Wildlife Department, Resources Protection Division. 16 p.

Mirowsky, K.M. 1997. Bats in palms: precarious habitat. Bats. 15: 3-6.

Mirowsky, K.M.; Horner, P.A.; Maxey, R.W.; Smith, S.A. 2004. Distributional records and roosts of southeastern myotis and Rafinesque's big-eared bat in eastern Texas. Southwestern Naturalist. 49: 294-298.

Mount, R.H. 1986. Vertebrates of Alabama in need of special attention. Auburn, AL: Auburn University. 45 p.

Mumford, R.E.; Whitaker, J.O., Jr. 1975. Seasonal activity of bats at an Indiana cave. In: Proceedings, Indiana Academy of Science. 84: 500-507.

Mumford, R.E.; Whitaker, J.O., Jr. 1982. Mammals of Indiana. Terre Haute, IN: Indiana University Press. 537 p.

NatureServe. 2002. NatureServe Explorer: an online encyclopedia of life [Web application]. Version 4.1. http://www.natureserve.org.

Reidinger, R.F., Jr.; Cockrum, E.L. 1978. Organochlorine residues in free-tailed bats (*Tadarida brasiliensis*) at Eagle Creek Cave, Greenlee County, Arizona. In: Proceedings, Fourth International Bat Research Conference. Nairobi, Kenya: Kenya Literature Bureau: 85-96.

Rhoads, S.N. 1897. A new southeastern race of the little brown bat. Proceedings, Academy of Natural Science, Philadelphia. 49: 227-228.

Rice, D.W. 1955. Life history and ecology of *Myotis austroriparius* in Florida. Gainesville, FL: University of Florida. 74 p. Ph.D. dissertation.

Rice, D.W. 1957. Life history and ecology of *Myotis austroriparius* in Florida. Journal of Mammalogy. 38(1): 15-32.

Saugey, D.A.; Heath, D.R.; Heigt, G.A. 1989. The bats of the Ouachita Mountains. In: Proceedings, Arkansas Academy of Science. 43: 71-77.

Saugey, D.A.; McDaniel, V.R.; Rowe, M.C.; Engl, D.R.; Chandler-Mozisek, L.R.; Cochran, B.G. 1993. Arkansas range extensions of the eastern small-footed bat (*Myotis leibii*) and northern long-eared bat (*Myotis septentrionalis*) and additional county records for the silver-haired bat (*Lasionycteris noctivagans*), hoary bat (*Lasiurus cinereus*), southeastern bat (*Myotis austroriparius*), and Rafinesque's big-eared bat (*Plecotus rafinesquii*). In: Proceedings, Arkansas Academy of Science. 47: 102-106.

Schmidly, D.J.; Wilkens, K.T.; Weyn, B.C.; Honeycutt, R.L. 1977. The bats of east Texas. Texas Journal of Science. 28: 127-143.

Sealander, J.A. 1979. A guide to Arkansas mammals. Conway, AR: River Road Press. 313 p.

Sheffield, S.R.; Chapman, B.R. 1992. First records of mammals from McCurtain County, Oklahoma. Texas Journal of Science. 44: 491-492.

Sherman, H.B. 1930. Birth of the young of *Myotis austroriparius*. Journal of Mammalogy. 11: 495-503.

Sherman, H.B. 1939. Notes on the food of some Florida bats. Journal of Mammalogy. 20: 103-104.

Stevenson, D.; Tuttle, M.D. 1982. Growth and survival of bats. In: Kunz, T.H., ed. Ecology of bats. New York: Plenum. 425 p.

Tuttle, M.D. 1975. Population ecology of the gray bat (*Myotis grisescens*): factors influencing early growth and development. Occas. Pap. 36. Lawrence, KS: University of Kansas, Museum of Natural History. 36: 1-24.

Tuttle, M.D. 1981. Gating as a means of protecting cave dwelling bats. In: Stitt, R., ed. Cage gating: a handbook. 2nd ed., rev. Huntsdale, AL: National Speleological Society: 40-45.

Tuttle, M.D.; Taylor, D.A. 1995. Bats and mines. Bat Conservation International Research Publication. 3: 41.

U.S. Department of Agriculture, Forest Service. 2003. Forest Inventory and Analysis. 98 p.

U.S. Fish & Wildlife Service (USFWS). 1983. Recovery plan for the Indiana bat (revision). Washington, DC: U.S. Fish & Wildlife Service. 83 p.

USFWS. 1989. U.S. Fish & Wildlife Service, endangered and threatened wildlife and plants; animal notice of review. Federal Register. 54: 554-579.

USFWS. 1996. U.S. Fish & Wildlife Service, endangered and threatened wildlife and plants; notice of final decision on identification of candidates for listing as endangered or threatened. Federal Register. 61: 64481-64485.

Walker, C.W.; Sandel, J.K.; Honeycutt, R.L.; Adams, C. 1996. Winter utilization of box culverts by vespertilionid bats in southeast Texas. Texas Journal of Science. 48: 166-168.

Webster, W.D.; Colwell, P.B.; Shields, M.A. 1984. Noteworthy records of mammals from North Carolina. Journal of the Elisha Mitchell Scientific Society. 100(3): 112-115.

Wenner, A.S. 1984. Current status and management of gray bat caves in Jackson County, Florida. Florida Field Naturalist. 12: 1-12.

Whitaker, J.O.; Brack, J.V.; Cope, J.B. 2002. Are bats in Indiana declining? In: Proceedings, Indiana Academy of Science. 111: 95-106.

Wilhide, J.D. 2001. Personal communication. Professor of wildlife ecology, Arkansas State University, Jonesboro, Arkansas. Conversation.

Zinn, T.L. 1977. Community ecology of Florida bats with emphasis on *Myotis austroriparius*. Gainesville, FL: University of Florida. 87 p. M.S. thesis.

Zinn, T.L.; Humphrey, S.R. 1981. Seasonal food resources and prey selection of the southeastern brown bat (*Myotis austroriparius*) in Florida. Florida Scientist. 44(2): 81-90.

Conservation Assessment: *Myotis leibii* (Eastern Small-Footed Myotis) in the Eastern United States

Sybill Amelon[1] **and Dirk Burhans**[2]

Taxonomy and Nomenclature

The eastern small-footed myotis [*Myotis leibii* (Audubon and Bachman 1842) (f. G. *mys* mouse; and *otis* ear, and *leibii* in honor of G.C. Leib who collected the type specimen; i.e., Leib's mouse-eared bat)] belongs to the class Mammalia, order Chiroptera, family Vespertilionidae, subfamily Vespertilioninae, genus/species *Myotis leibii* (Miller and Allen 1928). *M. leibii* is considered monotypic (Best and Jennings 1997). This species also has been identified by different common names: Leib's bat (Audubon and Bachman 1842), least brown bat (Mohr 1934), and Leib's masked bat or least bat (Hitchcock 1949).

Type location for the *Vespertilio leibii* (Audubon and Bachman 1842: 284) is Erie County, Michigan (=Ohio—Miller and Allen 1928: 172). Type location for the *M. winnemana* (Nelson 1913: 183) is Plummers Island (=Montgomery County, Maryland—Hall 1981: 188).

Notes on Taxonomy

The *M. leibii* taxonomy has been confusing (Best and Jennings 1997; Glass and Baker 1965, 1968). The epithet "*subulatus*" was used as *M. subulatus leibii* (Miller and Allen 1928); *M. subulatus* was also used for *M. ciliolabrum,* a western species considered a subspecies of *M. leibii.* Based on morphometric measurements of the cranium (Audubon and Bachman 1842; van Zyll de Jong 1984, 1985), the western population is recognized as *M. ciliolabrum* and the eastern population as *M. leibii.* Addi-

tional biochemical evidence (Herd 1987) supported the conclusion that they are distinct species. Jones et al. (1992) listed these species as distinct; however, Wilson and Reeder (1993) did not. Best and Jennings (1997) followed Jones et al. (1992) and considered *M. leibii* monotypic.

Description of Species

Myotis leibii is the smallest Myotis in the Eastern United States. Characteristic measurements include wingspan, 212 to 248 millimeters (mm); total length, 72 to 84 mm; tail length, 30 to 39 mm; hindfoot, 6 to 8 mm and less than one-half as long as the tibia; ear, less than 15 mm and exceeds the length of the nose when laid forward; forearm, 30 to 36 mm; and skull, 12.3 to 13.3 mm. The braincase is somewhat flattened; the forehead slopes gradually from the rostrum, in contrast to that in other members of the genus. Weight ranges from 3 to 8 grams (g) (mean summer weight 3.8 g) (Banfield 1974, Hamilton and Whitaker 1979, Schwartz and Schwartz 1981). The sexes of *M. leibii* are similar. Females have two mammae. The face, ears, wings, and interfemoral membranes are very dark brown to black. The dark face and ears appear as a mask. Pelage color varies dorsally from pale yellowish brown to golden brown; ventrally, pelage is paler. The hairs of the back are bi-colored—very dark at the roots and pale at the ends—giving the back a yellowish-brown appearance. The base of the interfemoral membrane and the undersurface of the wings are sparsely furred. The tragus is long and pointed; the calcar has a prominent keel. The skull is short with a broad rostrum. The dental formula is i 2/3, c 1/1, p 3/3, m 3/3, total 38 (Best and Jennings 1997, Hamilton and Whitaker 1979).

[1] Wildlife biologist, U.S. Department of Agriculture, Forest Service, North Central Research Station, Columbia, MO.

[2] Postdoctoral associate, Department of Fisheries and Wildlife Science, University of Missouri, Columbia, MO.

Biology, Life History, and Natural History

Reproductive Biology and Phenology

Little information about reproduction of *M. leibii* has been published. *M. leibii* is thought to be similar to sympatric *Myotis* that breed in the fall; spermatozoa are stored in the uterus of hibernating females until spring ovulation and a single pup is born in May or June (Barbour and Davis 1969, Godin 1977, Hamilton and Whitaker 1979, Merritt 1987). Little is known about the development and survival of *M. leibii* young. Anecdotal evidence suggests females fly with newborns as early as June (Hobson 1998). Small maternity and nursery colonies of *M. leibii* have been reported in vacant or little-used buildings (Barbour and Davis 1969, Merritt 1987, Harvey et al. 1999b), behind loose bark in trees, and in crevasses on bridges, all of which were significantly exposed to sunlight (MacGregor 2002, Tuttle 1964). Maternity colonies were also located under exposed rocks on open ridges and in the expansion joint of a concrete bridge (MacGregor et al. 1999).

In Arkansas, a reproductively active male was observed on September 14 (Saugey et al. 1993), which is consistent with sympatric *Myotis* species that breed in the fall. Males may roost singly or in small groups (Barbour and Davis 1969) and may roost in sandstone rock shelters, on cliffs, in caves, and even in trees (MacGregor 2002). In Kentucky, males have been captured at the entrances of abandoned mines, railroad tunnels, and caves during the breeding season (MacGregor 2002).

Hitchcock (1965) and Mohr (1952) reported sex ratios of 1:1 at birth. Survival is reported to be greater for males (0.75) than for females (0.42); the additional burden of pregnancy to thermoregulation is a potential cause of lower survival in females (Hitchcock 1965, Hitchcock et al. 1984).

Ecology and Behavior

M. leibii is one of the rarest bats in North America (Barbour and Davis 1969; Griffin 1940; Mohr 1934, 1952; Davis et al. 1965; Gates et al. 1984). The species has been encountered most frequently during fall swarming activities and hibernation (Barbour and Davis 1969, Hitchcock 1949, Krutzsch 1966, McDaniel et al. 1982). Very little is known about the ecology and life history of this species. Concerning the Mammoth

Cave region of Kentucky, Barbour and Davis (1969) reported, "*M. leibii* is fairly common in late summer flocks of migrating bats. The whereabouts of these individuals at other seasons is unknown."

In open habitats, *M. leibii* emits frequency-modulated (FM) echolocation calls that range from approximately 45 to 80 kilohertz (kHz) and each has a duration of just under 3 milliseconds (ms). Based on echolocation design and morphological characteristics of wingtip shape and aspect ratio, characteristics of foraging locations indicate high levels of vegetative clutter (Norberg and Raynor 1987).

M. leibii is reported to be among the hardiest of bats with respect to winter temperatures and hibernation (Harvey et al. 1981). This species is one of the last to enter hibernacula, seldom entering before mid-November (Godin 1977, Gunier and Elder 1973) and often departing by early March (Hicks 2002, Mohr 1936). *M. leibii* inhabit hilly or mountainous areas and has been found at elevations of 300 to 780 meters (m) in Pennsylvania (Mohr 1932), 750 m in Virginia (Johnson 1950), 1,125 m in Kentucky (Barbour 1951), and 675 m in Georgia (Baker 1967, Baker and Patton 1967). This species often is found in drafty locations near the openings of hibernacula where the temperature may drop below freezing and humidity is relatively low (Fenton 1972).

Obligate associations with other species have not been observed. *M. leibii* has been observed roosting in the same hibernacula with *Eptesicus fuscus, Pipistrellus subflavus, M. lucifugus, M. septentrionalis, M. sodalis*, and *Corynorhinus rafinesquii* (Butchkowski 2001, Harvey 1989, Schwartz 1954, Sealander 1979, Tuttle 1964, Saugey et al. 1993).

Hibernation

M. leibii appears to be an obligate hibernator, usually roosting singly or in small clusters (Fenton 1972, Schwartz 1954, Stihler and Brack 1977, Harvey et al. 1991). The largest hibernating cluster was reported from Ontario, where 142 individuals were clustered on 26 February (Hitchcock 1949). Periods of activity observed during hibernation suggest this species may not spend as much time in deep torpor as do other cave-hibernating species (Hitchcock 1946, Mohr 1936, Tuttle 1964).

Food Habits

M. leibii is insectivorous and feeds on flying insects. This species forages mainly over water, emerging shortly after sunset. These bats can fill their stomachs within an hour of emerging. They reportedly fly slowly and distinctly at all levels of the understory and canopy but usually stay within 1 to 3 m of the ground (Barbour and Davis 1969, Harvey 1999, Harvey et al. 1999b, Linzey 1998, Merritt 1987).

Mortality and Predation Factors

Available information indicates that in most areas of its range, *M. leibii* spends at least the coldest portions of the year in hibernacula, primarily in caves and mines. Mortality from vandalism, alteration of hibernation sites, disturbance, and natural events such as floods is likely to occur as has been documented for other Myotis species. Predators would be expected to be similar to those documented for similar species, including snakes, owls, hawks, raccoons, foxes, and domestic cats. Endoparasites and ectoparasites are expected to be similar to those found on similar bat species (Mumford and Whitaker 1975, Whitaker and Loomis 1979, Whitaker and Mumford 1973); they include mites and chiggers.

Longevity

A single longevity record for *M. leibii* exists. An individual bat is reported to have lived 12 years (Hitchcock 1965).

Banding Data and Site Fidelity

Mohr (1936) found marked bats in the same cave in different seasons. Attempts to relocate these bats to alternative roosts resulted in their return to the original locations of their capture, suggesting some degree of site fidelity.

Distribution

The current range of *M. leibii* is from Ontario and Quebec through New England then southward to Georgia and Alabama and west to Oklahoma, Arkansas, and Missouri, generally following the eastern mountain ranges (fig. 1). *M. leibii* has been documented in 125 hibernacula across southeastern Canada and the Eastern United States. Most of the occurrences

Figure 1. *The distribution of* Myotis leibii.

* = Isolated or questionable records.
Source: Bat Conservation International 2003, http://www.batcon.org.

have been documented in New York, Pennsylvania, West Virginia, and Virginia. Historically, this species has always been considered fairly rare with patchy distribution where it is found (Barbour and Davis 1969).

Habitat Requirements

Maternity Period (May to August)

Roosting Habitat

The habitat for *M. leibii* is mostly in hilly or mountainous terrain where the geology provides fractures and cracks in exposed rock or in karst areas. Summer roost sites include caves, mines (Fenton 1972), buildings (Hitchcock 1955), rocks on exposed ridges, cracks in rock faces, outcrops (Harvey et al. 1991, Kiser 2001), and bridges (MacGregor 2002). Tuttle (1964) reported two individuals under a rock near a rock quarry in April in Tennessee. Barbour and Davis (1969), while hunting for snakes, discovered an individual under a stone on a hillside in Missouri. *M. leibii* has been observed resting in limestone caves in spring and summer in Virginia (Krutzsch 1966). Several accounts have found this species roosting in human-made structures, including houses, barns, and bridges (MacGregor and Kiser 1998, Harvey et al. 1999a). Proximity to water may be a factor in maternity roost locations (MacGregor and Kiser 1998).

Foraging Habitat
M. leibii has been observed foraging over ponds and streams (MacGregor and Kiser 1998).

Hibernation Period (October to April)
M. leibii uses caves, mines, and rock crevices as hibernation sites in winter where they can be found in narrow crevices, under rocks on the floor, in human-made tunnels, or in cracks in the wall or ceiling (McDaniel et al. 1982). This species usually hibernates singly but may be found in small groups with other members of its species or other species (Fenton 1972). The small size of these bats enables them to push into very small crevices and in breakdown areas of mines or caves, where it may be difficult to observe or count (Saugey et al. 1989). This species is believed to fly outside the hibernation site in winter (Hitchcock 1965, Schwartz 1954) and to accept full gates on the caves or mines it uses for hibernation (Currie 1999). *M. leibii* frequently hibernate horizontally instead of vertically (Butchkowski 2001, Godin 1977, Martin 1966, Stihler 2001). The eastern small-footed myotis seems to be more tolerant of temperature extremes and is commonly seen very close to cave or mine entrances where air temperatures can vary greatly and humidity is relatively low (Barbour and Davis 1969, Merritt 1987, Harvey et al. 1991). Fenton (1972) found *M. leibii* to arouse from torpor below –9 °C compared to –4 °C for *M. lucifugus*. Loss of mass during hibernation from December to April was approximately 16 percent of body weight.

Potential Threats

Natural or Human Factors
Disturbance during the hibernation or maternity periods is a significant factor in the widespread decline of cave- and mine-dependent bat species (Clark 1988b, Currie 1999). The main factor leading to population declines is destruction of roost sites, particularly hibernacula (Humphrey 1978, Sheffield and Chapman 1992). North American bat conservation efforts have,

therefore, focused primarily on protecting hibernacula from vandalism and physical alterations.

Food chain poisoning by pesticides—in particular insecticides such as organochlorines and anticholinesterase—has been demonstrated to negatively impact insectivorous bats (Clark 1988a, 2001; Cockrum 1952, 1970; Reidinger and Cockrum 1978; Clark et al. 1986; Fleming et al. 1983). Bat population declines have been attributed to pesticide poisoning (Brady et al. 1982, Geluso 1976, Reidinger 1976, Tuttle 1979), chemical pollution (Tuttle 1979), siltation of waterways (Tuttle 1979), flooding (Hall 1962), and disturbance by humans (Fenton 1972, Humphrey 1978, Tuttle 1977, Brady et al. 1982, Fenton et al. 1980, Speakman et al. 1991).

Present or Potential Risks to Habitat
One major threat to *M. leibii* is the lack of knowledge about its life history needs and population status. Because of its propensity for mines and loose rock materials, this species may be threatened by activities related to mining and surface rock disturbance. Mines in several States are subject to closure, collapse, natural events such as flooding, or human disturbances. Widespread recreational use of caves, causing indirect and direct disturbances by humans during the hibernation period, poses the greatest known threat to this species. Altering cave and mine microclimates by modifying airflow patterns may pose a threat to this species. Because of its very small size and its association with mining activities, this species may be particularly vulnerable to pesticides, heavy metal accumulations, and environmental contaminants.

Inadequacy of Existing Regulatory Mechanisms
A lack of information about the population status of *M. leibii* may preclude it from necessary protection. Early bat roost protection efforts focused on eliminating or reducing human disturbances during critical hibernation and maternity periods by installing informative signs or "bat friendly" gates and fences. In some cases, these efforts were unfavorable because of limited understanding of bat behavior and cave microclimate factors. Protecting natural and human-made roosting structures is one of the highest priorities in all recovery plans for listed species. Funding and access to facilitate these protection measures are often unavailable.

Population Status

Rangewide

Both Global Heritage Status and National Heritage Status are "3," indicating this species is rare to uncommon (NatureServe 2002). Individual State Heritage Status is described in State Summaries and in table 1. *M. leibii* is considered rare or uncommon throughout its range (Choate et al. 1994). This species was a former C2 candidate.

Habitat Status

Summary of Land Ownership and Existing Habitat Protection

National Forests

Estimates of the potential available habitat for *M. leibii* were based on U.S. Department of Agriculture (USDA) Forest Service Forest Inventory and Analysis (FIA) data, which estimate the amount of upland hardwood and pine-hardwood forest land more than 60 years old for all States with national forests in Regions 8 and 9 (Southern and Eastern Forest Service Regions combined to look at the entire species range) and Region 9 (examined alone to look at potential available habitat for States in the Eastern Region), excluding rarely used deciduous forest types such as aspen. This coarse-scale assessment of habitat availability considers forest type and age class based on USDA Forest Service FIA data (USDA Forest Service 2003); this analysis does not consider other aspects of forest structure that may influence use by this species. The database used is subject to sampling errors associated with coarse-scale inventory. Estimates were for the acreage of upland hardwood and pine-hardwood forest land for forests of all ownerships, including other federally owned, State-owned, county/municipal-owned, and privately owned lands within these States. Approximately 3.8 percent of upland hardwood, bottom-land hardwood, and pine-hardwood forest types occurs on National Forest System (NFS) lands within the range of this species; less than 1 percent occurs on NFS lands within Region 9. Of the potential habitat for this species, 90 percent occurs on

privately owned lands (figs. 2 and 5). Estimates indicate that 347,529,086 acres of upland hardwood, bottom-land hardwood, and pine-hardwood forest land that could potentially serve as roosting and foraging habitat occur within the range of this species. Estimates also indicate that stands more than 60 years old in upland hardwood, bottom-land hardwood, and pine-hardwood forest types would provide suitable trees to meet the roosting requirements of this species. Within the range of *M. leibii*, estimates indicate that 93,673,155 acres, or 27 percent of the total available, are more than 60 years old (figs. 3 and 4). On NFS lands within Region 9, estimates show that 11,359,361 acres of habitat (upland hardwood, bottom-land hardwood, and pine-hardwood forest types) and 3,925,418 acres of upland hardwood and pine-hardwood forest types more than 60 years old (34.5 percent) are available for roosting and foraging (figs. 3 and 4).

To date, reports from hibernacula counts indicate this species uses at least 125 caves or mines; *M. leibii* are usually present in these caves or mines in very low numbers. Of the available hibernacula count data, the highest numbers of hibernating individuals were reported from two sites in New York.

Figure 2. *Ownership of upland hardwood, bottom-land hardwood, and pine-hardwood forest types within States overlapping the range of* M. leibii.

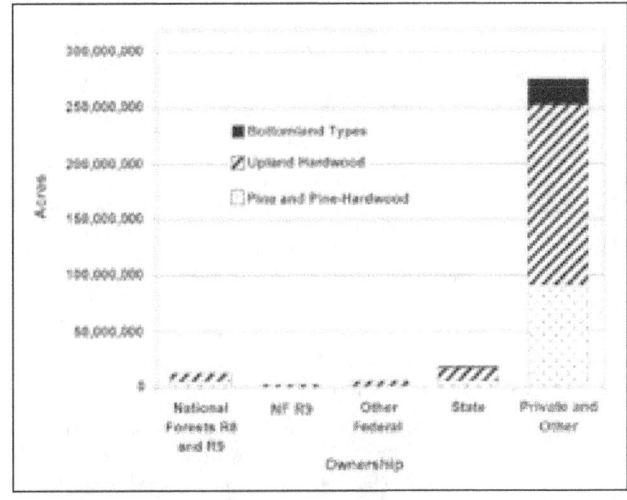

Alabama, Arkansas, Connecticut, Delaware, Georgia, Indiana, Kentucky, Maine, Maryland, Massachusetts, Missouri, New Hampshire, New Jersey, New York, North Carolina, Ohio, Oklahoma, Pennsylvania, South Carolina, Tennessee, Vermont, Virginia, West Virginia.

Figure 3. *Acreage by ownership of upland hardwood forest type and percentage of upland hardwood forest type more than 60 years old by ownership within States overlapping the range of* M. leibii.

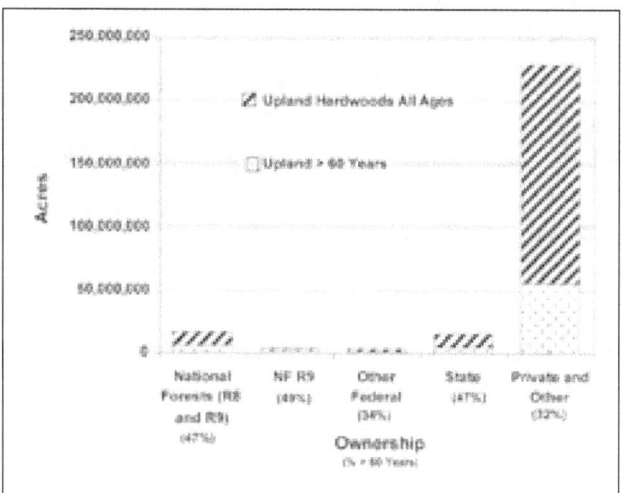

Alabama, Arkansas, Connecticut, Delaware, Georgia, Indiana, Kentucky, Maine, Maryland, Massachusetts, Missouri, New Hampshire, New Jersey, New York, North Carolina, Ohio, Oklahoma, Pennsylvania, South Carolina, Tennessee, Vermont, Virginia, West Virginia.

Figure 4. *Acreage by ownership of pine and pine-hardwood forest types and percentage of pine and pine-hardwood forest types more than 60 years old by ownership within States overlapping the range of* M. leibii.

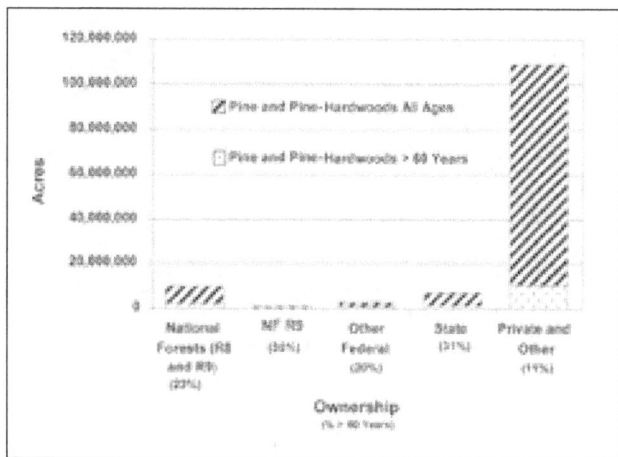

Alabama, Arkansas, Connecticut, Delaware, Georgia, Indiana, Kentucky, Maine, Maryland, Massachusetts, Missouri, New Hampshire, New Jersey, New York, North Carolina, Ohio, Oklahoma, Pennsylvania, South Carolina, Tennessee, Vermont, Virginia, West Virginia.

Figure 5. *Acreage by ownership of bottom-land hardwood forest type and percentage of bottom-land hardwood forest type more than 60 years old by ownership within States overlapping the range of* M. leibii.

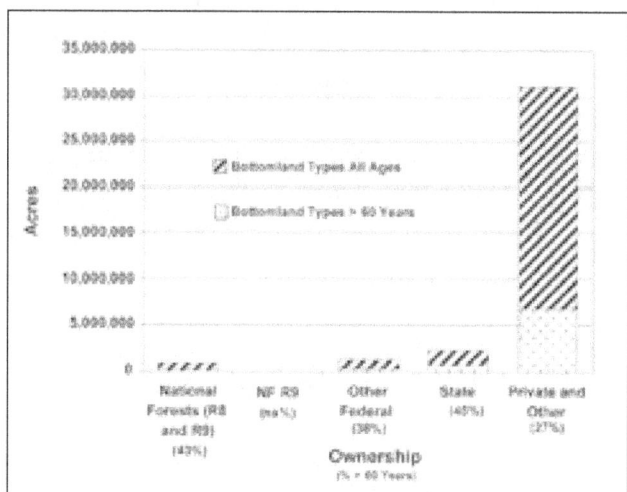

Alabama, Arkansas, Connecticut, Delaware, Georgia, Indiana, Kentucky, Maine, Maryland, Massachusetts, Missouri, New Hampshire, New Jersey, New York, North Carolina, Ohio, Oklahoma, Pennsylvania, South Carolina, Tennessee, Vermont, Virginia, West Virginia.

State Summaries

Missouri. State status is undetermined (SU, table 1). The distribution and activity of bats on the Mark Twain National Forest were studied in the summer and fall between 1997 and 2003. Surveys sampled upland flyways and ponds and riparian areas; *M. leibii* accounted for less than 1 percent of bats captured each year (Amelon 2001).

New Hampshire. State status is extremely rare (S1, table 1).

New York. State status is very rare (S2, table 1). *M. leibii* are found near entrances of mines and caves during hibernation and associated with talus areas in summer surveys.

Ohio. State status is undetermined (SH, table 1).

Pennsylvania. State status is extremely rare (S1, table 1). An analysis of mammals in Pennsylvania based on population status, habitat, and threats ranked *M. leibii* as rare (Kirkland and Krim 1990). Dunn and Hall (1989) noted that 52 percent of

Table 1. *Population status of* Myotis leibii *by State[1].*

State	Status[2]	Summer habitat (reported)	Winter habitat (reported)
Alabama	S1		
Arkansas	S1		Caves and mines
Delaware	SU		
Georgia	S2		
Indiana	NA[a]		Caves and mines
Kentucky	S2	Buildings, bridges, caves, mines, rock outcrops, and trees	Caves and mines
Maine	S1		
Maryland	S1		
Massachusetts	S1[a]		
Missouri	SU	Glades and rock outcrops	Caves and mines
New Hampshire	S1[b]		Caves and mines
New Jersey	S1		
New York	S2[a]	Bridges	Caves and mines
North Carolina	SU	Rocky structures, cliffs, and bridges	Caves, mines, and rock shelters
Ohio	SH[a]		
Oklahoma	S1		
Pennsylvania	S1[b]	Deciduous mixed forest, talus slopes, and hemlock forest	Caves, mines, and rock outcrops
South Carolina	S1		
Tennessee	S2	Under rocks, trees, and buildings	
Vermont	S1[c]		Caves and mines
Virginia	S1		
West Virginia	S1	Caves, rock outcrops, talus slopes, and rock shelters	Caves and mines

[a] State Listed Species of Concern.

[b] State Listed Endangered.

[c] State Listed Threatened.

[1] Information about population and habitat use is based on literature cited. See text and References section.

[2] Status based on Natural Heritage State Rarity ranks (NatureServe 2002). S1: Extremely rare; usually five or fewer occurrences in the State, or, in the case of communities, covering less than 50 hectares (ha) in aggregate; or may have a few remaining individuals; often especially vulnerable to extirpation. S2: Very rare; usually between 5 and 20 occurrences, or, in the case of communities, covering less than 250 ha in aggregate; or few occurrences with many individuals; often susceptible to becoming endangered. SH: Historically known from the State but not verified for an extended period (usually more than 15 years); this rank is used primarily when inventory has been attempted recently. SNR/SU: Status not ranked/Status uncertain, often because of low search effort or cryptic nature of the element.

Pennsylvania hibernacula were small caves of less than 150 m (500 feet) in length. Habitat is mostly in hilly or mountainous areas, in or near deciduous or evergreen forest, and sometimes in mostly open farmland. In Pennsylvania, Mohr (1932) found this species mostly in heavy hemlock forests in the foothills of mountains that rise to 2,000 feet (600 m).

Vermont. State status is extremely rare (S1, table 1). Reported only in Bennington, Orange, Rutland, and Windsor Counties.

West Virginia. State status is extremely rare (S1, table 1). *M. leibii* has been seen resting in limestone caves in West Virginia in spring and summer (Krutzsch 1966). Existence of *M. leibii* has been reported in Fayette, Grant, Greenbrier, Hardy, Mercer, Monongalia, Monroe, Morgan, Nicholas, Pendleton, Pocahontas, Preston, Randolph, Tucker, and Webster Counties.

References

Amelon, S.K. 2001. Unpublished data. Columbia, MO: U.S. Department of Agriculture, Forest Service, North Central Research Station.

Audubon, J.J.; Bachman, J. 1842. Descriptions of new species of quadrupeds inhabiting North America. Journal of Academy of Natural Sciences of Philadelphia. 8: 280-323.

Baker, R.J.; Patton, J.L. 1967. Karyotypes and karyotypic variation of North American vespertilionid bats. Journal of Mammalogy. 48: 270-286.

Baker, W.W. 1967. *Myotis leibii* in Georgia. Journal of Mammalogy. 48: 142.

Banfield, A.W.F. 1974. The mammals of Canada. Toronto, Canada: University of Toronto Press. 438 p.

Barbour, R.W. 1951. The mammals of Big Black Mountain, Harlan County, Kentucky. Journal of Mammalogy. 32: 100-110.

Barbour, R.W.; Davis, W.H. 1969. Bats of America. Lexington, KY: University of Kentucky Press. 286 p.

Best, T.L.; Jennings, J.B. 1997. *Myotis leibii*. Mammalian Species. 547: 1-6.

Brady, J.T.; Kunz, T.H.; Tuttle, M.D.; Wilson, D.E. 1982. Gray bat recovery plan. Denver, CO: U.S. Fish & Wildlife Service. 91 p.

Butchkowski, C. 2001. Personal communication. Nongame wildlife biologist, Pennsylvania Department of Fish and Wildlife, Barree, Pennsylvania. Conversation.

Choate, J.R.; Jones, J.K.; Jones, J.C. 1994. Handbook of mammals of the South-Central States. Baton Rouge, LA: Louisiana State University Press. 336 p.

Clark, D.R., Jr. 1988a. Environmental contaminants and the management of bat populations in the United States. In: Proceedings, symposium on management of amphibians, reptiles, and small mammals in North America. Laurel, MD: U.S. Fish & Wildlife Service: 409-413.

Clark, D.R., Jr. 1988b. How sensitive are bats to insecticides? Wildlife Society Bulletin. 16: 399-403.

Clark, D.R., Jr. 2001. DDT and the decline of free-tailed bats (*Tadarida brasiliensis*) at Carlsbad Caverns, New Mexico. Archives of Environmental Contamination and Toxicology. 40: 537-543.

Clark, D.R., Jr.; Shapiro, W.A.; John, F.M. 1986. Metal residues in bat colonies, Jackson County, Florida, 1981-1983. Florida Field Naturalist. 14: 38-45.

Cockrum, E.L. 1952. Longevity in the pipistrelle, *Pipistrellus subflavus subflavus*. Journal of Mammalogy. 33: 491-492.

Cockrum, E.L. 1970. Insecticides and guano bats. Ecology. 51: 761-762.

Currie, R.R. 1999. An overview of the response of bats to protection efforts. In: Proceedings, Indiana Bat Symposium. Lexington, KY: Bat Conservation International. 24 p.

Davis, W.H.; Hassell, M.D.; Rippy, C.L. 1965. *Myotis leibii leibii* in Kentucky. Journal of Mammalogy. 46: 683-684.

Dunn, J.P.; Hall, J.S. 1989. Status of cave-dwelling bats in Pennsylvania, USA. Journal of the Pennsylvania Academy of Science. 63(3): 166-172.

Fenton, M.B. 1972. Distribution and overwintering of *Myotis leibii* and *Eptesicus fuscus* in Ontario. Life Sci. Occas. Pap. 21. Ontario, Canada: Royal Ontario Museum: 1-8.

Fenton, M.B.; van Zyll de Jong, C.G.; Bell, G.P.; Campbell, D.B.; Laplante, L. 1980. Distribution, parturition, and feeding of bats in south central British Columbia. Canadian Field Naturalist. 94(4): 416-420.

Fleming, W.J.; Clark, D.R., Jr.; Henny, C.J. 1983. Organochlorine pesticides and PCBs: a continuing problem for the 1980s. Environmental contamination, toxicity and wildlife conference. [unknown]:186-199.

Gates, J.E.; Feldhammer, G.A.; Raesly, R.L.; Griffith, L.A. 1984. Status of cave-dwelling bats in Maryland: importance of marginal habitats. Wildlife Society Bulletin. 12: 162-169.

Geluso, K. 1976. Bat mortality: pesticide poisoning and migratory stress. Science. 194: 184-186.

Glass, B.P.; Baker, R.J. 1965. *Vespertilio subulatus* Say, 1823: proposed suppression under the plenary powers (Mammalia: Chiroptera). The Bulletin of Zoological Nomenclature. 22: 204-205.

Glass, B.P.; Baker, R.J. 1968. The status of the name *Myotis subulatus* Say. Proceedings, Biological Society of Washington. 81: 257-260.

Godin, A.J. 1977. Wild mammals of New England. Baltimore, MD: Johns Hopkins University Press. 304 p.

Griffin, D.R. 1940. Notes on the life histories of New England cave bats. Journal of Mammalogy. 21: 181-187.

Gunier, W.J.; Elder, W.H. 1973. New records of *Myotis leibii* from Missouri. American Midland Naturalist. 89: 489-490.

Hall, J.S. 1962. A life history and taxonomic study of the Indiana bat, *Myotis sodalis*. Reading Public Museum and Art Gallery, Science Publication. 12: 1-68.

Hamilton, W.J.; Whitaker, J.O., Jr. 1979. Mammals of the Eastern United States. Ithaca, NY: Cornell University Press. 346 p.

Harvey, M.J. 1989. Endangered bats of Arkansas: monitoring population and status at major hibernacula and summer caves. Government Report/Document Arkansas Game and Fish Commission. 52 p.

Harvey, M.J. 1999. Eastern bat species of concern to mining. Unpublished paper. Cookeville, TN: Tennessee Tech University. 4 p.

Harvey, M.J.; Altenback, J.S.; Best, T.L. 1999a. Bats of the United States. Little Rock, AR: Arkansas Game and Fish Commission. 64 p.

Harvey, M.J.; Cassidy, J.J.; O'Hagan, G.G. 1981. Endangered bats of Arkansas: distribution, status and ecology and management. Memphis, TN: Memphis State University. 56 p.

Harvey, M.J.; MacGregor, J.R.; Currie, R.R. 1991. Distribution and status of Chiroptera in Kentucky and Tennessee. Journal of the Tennessee Academy of Science. 4: 191-193.

Harvey, M.J.; McDaniel, V.R.; Wilhide, J.D. 1999b. Behavioral ecology of endangered bats in Arkansas, 1993-1999. Little Rock, AR: Arkansas Game and Fish Commission. 118 p.

Herd, R.M. 1987. Electrophoretic divergence of *Myotis leibii* and *myotis Ciliolabrum* (Chiroptera: Vespertilionidae). Canadian Journal of Zoology. 65: 1857-1860.

Hicks, A. 2002. Personal communication. Wildlife biologist, New York State Department of Environmental Conservation. Conversation.

Hitchcock, H.B. 1946. *Myotis subulatus leibii* in Ontario. Journal of Mammalogy. 26: 433.

Hitchcock, H.B. 1949. Hibernation of bats in southeastern Ontario and adjacent Quebec. Canadian Field Naturalist. 63: 47-59.

Hitchcock, H.B. 1955. A summer colony of the least bat, *Myotis subulatus leibii* (Audubon and Bachman). Canadian Field Naturalist. 69(2): 31.

Hitchcock, H.B. 1965. Twenty-three years of bat banding in Ontario and Quebec. Canadian Field Naturalist. 79: 4-14.

Hitchcock, H.B.; Keen, R.; Kurta, A. 1984. Survival rates of *Myotis leibii* and *Eptesicus fuscus* in southeastern Ontario. Journal of Mammalogy. 65(1): 126-130.

Hobson, C.S. 1998. Summer distribution, status and ecology of bats in western Virginia. Cookeville, TN: Tennessee Tech University. 91 p. M.S. thesis.

Humphrey, S.R. 1978. Status, winter habitat, and management of the endangered Indiana bat, *Myotis sodalis*. Florida Scientist. 41: 65-76.

Johnson, D.H. 1950. *Myotis subulatus leibii* in Virginia. Journal of Mammalogy. 31: 197.

Jones, C.; Hoffmann, R.S.; Rice, D.W.; Jones, C.; Baker, R.J. 1992. Revised checklist of North American mammals north of Mexico. Occas. Pap. 146. Austin, TX: Museum of the Texas Technological University: 1-23.

Kirkland, G.L., Jr.; Krim, P.M. 1990. Survey of the statuses of the mammals of Pennsylvania. Journal of the Pennsylvania Academy of Science. 64(1): 33-45.

Kiser, J.D. 2001. Personal communication. Wildlife biologist, Daniel Boone National Forest, Lexington, KY. Conversation.

Krutzsch, P.H. 1966. Remarks on silver-haired and Leib's bat in Eastern United States. Journal of Mammalogy. 47: 121.

Linzey, D.W. 1998. The mammals of Virginia. Blacksburg, VA: McDonald and Woodward. 74 p.

MacGregor, J. 2002. Personal communication. State herpetologist, Kentucky Department of Fish and Wildlife. Phone conversation.

MacGregor, J.; Gumbert, J.M.; Reed, T.; Kiser, J. 1999. Autumn roosting habitat of Indiana bats: roost tree selection and use in response to natural disturbance, prescribed burning, and timber management on the Daniel Boone National Forest, Kentucky. Bat Research News, Abstract.

MacGregor, J.; Kiser, J. 1998. Recent reproductive records of eastern small-footed bat, *Myotis leibii* in Kentucky with notes on a maternity colony located in a concrete bridge. Bat Research News, Abstract.

Martin, R.L. 1966. Observations on hibernation of *Myotis subulatus*. Journal of Mammalogy. 47: 348-349.

McDaniel, V.R.; Harvey, M.J.; Tomlinson, C.R.; Page, K.N. 1982. Status of the bat *Myotis leibii* in Arkansas. Arkansas Academy of Science Proceedings. 36: 92-94.

Merritt, J.F. 1987. Guide to the mammals of Pennsylvania. Pittsburgh, PA: University of Pittsburgh. 44 p.

Miller, G.S.; Allen, G.M. 1928. The American bats of the genera *Myotis* and *Pizonyx*. Bulletin of the United States National Museum. 144: 1-218.

Mohr, C.E. 1932. *Myotis subulatus leibii* and *Myotis sodalis* in Pennsylvania. Journal of Mammalogy. 13: 160-161.

Mohr, C.E. 1934. Marking bats for later identification. Proceedings, Pennsylvania Academy of Science. 8: 26-30.

Mohr, C.E. 1936. Notes on the least brown bat *Myotis subulatus leibii*. Proceedings, Pennsylvania Academy of Science. 10: 62-65.

Mohr, C.E. 1952. A survey of bat banding in North America, 1932-1951. Bulletin National Speleological Society. 34: 33-47.

Mumford, R.E.; Whitaker, J.O. 1975. Seasonal activity of bats at an Indiana cave. In: Proceedings, Indiana Academy of Science. 84: 500-507.

NatureServe. 2002. NatureServe Explorer: an online encyclopedia of life [Web application]. Version 4.1. http://www.natureserve.org.

Norberg, U.M.; Raynor, J.M.V. 1987. Ecological morphology and flight in bats (Mammalia: Chiroptera): wing adaptations, flight performance, foraging strategy and echolocation. Philosophical Transactions, Royal Society of London. 316: 335-427.

Reidinger, R.F., Jr. 1976. Organochlorine residues in adults of six southwestern bat species. Journal of Wildlife Management. 40: 677-680.

Reidinger, R.F., Jr.; Cockrum, E.L. 1978. Organochlorine residues in free-tailed bats (*Tadarida brasiliensis*) at Eagle Creek Cave, Greenlee County, Arizona. In: Proceedings, Fourth International Bat Research Conference. Nairobi, Kenya: Kenya Literature Bureau: 85-96.

Saugey, D.A.; Heath, D.R.; Heigt, G.A. 1989. The bats of the Ouachita Mountains. In: Proceedings, Arkansas Academy of Science. 43: 71-77.

Saugey, D.A.; McDaniel, V.R.; Rowe, M.C.; Engl, D.R.; Chandler-Mozisek, L.R.; Cochran, B.G. 1993. Arkansas range extensions of the eastern small-footed bat (*Myotis leibii*) and northern long-eared bat (*Myotis septentrionalis*) and additional county records for the silver-haired bat (*Lasionycteris noctivagans*), hoary bat (*Lasiurus cinereus*), southeastern bat (*Myotis austroriparius*), and Rafinesque's big-eared bat (*Plecotus rafinesquii*). In: Proceedings, Arkansas Academy of Science. 47: 102-106.

Schwartz, A. 1954. A second record of *Myotis subulatus leibii* in North Carolina. Journal Elisha Mitchell Science Society. 70: 222.

Schwartz, C.W.; Schwartz, E.R. 1981. The wild mammals of Missouri. Columbia, MO: University of Missouri Press. 356 p.

Sealander, J.A. 1979. A guide to Arkansas mammals. Conway, AR: River Road Press. 313 p.

Sheffield, S.R.; Chapman, B.R. 1992. First records of mammals from McCurtain County, Oklahoma. Texas Journal of Science. 44: 491-492.

Speakman, J.; Racey, P.A.; Webb, P.I.; Catto, C.M.C.; Swift, S.M.; Burnett, A.M. 1991. Minimum summer populations and densities of bats in N.E. Scotland, near the northern borders of their distributions. Journal of Zoology London. 225: 327-345.

Stihler, C.W. 2001. Personal communication. Endangered species program leader, West Virginia Department of Natural Resources, Elkins, West Virginia. Conversation.

Stihler, C.W.; Brack, V. 1977. A survey of hibernating bats in Hellhole Cave, Pendleton County, West Virginia. Proceedings, West Virginia Academy of Science. 64(1): 34-35.

Tuttle, M.D. 1964. *Myotis subulatus* in Tennessee. Journal of Mammalogy. 45: 148-149.

Tuttle, M.D. 1977. Variation in the cave environment and its biological implications. National cave management symposium proceedings. Big Sky, MT: National Speleological Society: 108-121.

Tuttle, M.D. 1979. Status, causes of decline, and management of endangered gray bats. Journal of Wildlife Management. 43: 1-17.

U.S. Department of Agriculture, Forest Service. 2003. Forest Inventory and Analysis. 98 p.

van Zyll de Jong, C.G. 1984. Taxonomic relationships of Nearctic small-footed bats of the *Myotis leibii* group (Chiroptera: Vespertilionidae). Canadian Journal of Zoology. 62: 2519-2526.

van Zyll de Jong, C.G. 1985. Handbook of Canadian mammals: bats. Vol. 2. Ottawa: National Museums of Canada. 212 p.

Whitaker, J.O.; Loomis, R.B. 1979. Chiggers from the mammals of Indiana. In: Proceedings, Indiana Academy of Science. 88: 426-433.

Whitaker, J.O.; Mumford, R.E. 1973. External parasites of bats of Indiana. The Journal of Parasitology. 59: 1148-1150.

Wilson, D.E.; Reeder, T. 1993. Bat faunas: a trophic comparison. Systematic Zoology. 22: 14-29.

Conservation Assessment: *Myotis septentrionalis* (Northern Long-Eared Bat) in the Eastern United States

Sybill Amelon[1] and Dirk Burhans[2]

Taxonomy and Nomenclature

The northern long-eared bat [*Myotis septentrionalis* (Trouessart 1897) (f. G. *mys* mouse; *otis* ear; and L. *septentrionalis* northern; i.e., northern mouse-eared bat)] belongs to the class Mammalia, order Chiroptera, family Vespertilionidae, subfamily Vespertilioninae, genus/species *M. septentrionalis* (van Zyll de Jong 1979). Alternative common names include eastern long-eared bat and northern long-eared myotis. This species was previously identified as a subspecies of *M. keenii* (Miller and Allen 1928). *M. keenii* and *M. septentrionalis* occupy nonoverlapping ranges; thus, any reference to *M. keenii* outside the Pacific Northwest refers to *M. septentrionalis* (Caceres and Barclay 2000). No subspecies are recognized.

Alternative historic nomenclature includes the following:
- *Vespertilio gryphus var. septentrionalis*: Type location is Halifax, Nova Scotia (Trouessart 1897).
- *M. keenii septentrionalis* (Miller and Allen 1928: 105). Type location not stated.

Van Zyll de Jong (1979) proposed dividing *M. keenii* into two distinct species. Manning (1993) suggested that *M. keenii* and *M. septentrionalis* are sister species, whereas Nagorsen and Brigham (1993) argued that *M. evotis* and *M. septentrionalis* are sister species, based on external and cranial characteristics.

Description of Species

Myotis septentrionalis is a medium-sized bat of the Eastern United States and Canada. Characteristic measurements include wingspan, 228 to 258 millimeters (mm); total length, 77 to 100 mm; tail length, 35 to 48 mm; hindfoot, 8 to 10 mm (the hindfoot generally is less than 60 percent of the length of the tibia); ear, 14 to 19 mm; forearm, 34 to 39 mm; and skull, 14.6 to 15.6 mm. Weight ranges from 5 to 10 grams (g). Females are consistently heavier than males (Caire et al. 1979, Williams and Findley 1979). Pelage color dorsally is light brown or gray-brown; ventrally, pelage is sometimes a paler gray-brown to light gray. The wing membranes are of similar color to the dorsal pelage. A characteristic feature is the long ears that extend past the nose when laid forward. Juvenile pelage is duller than adult pelage. The tragus is straight, very long (10 to 12 mm), and distinctly pointed at the end. The calcar is not keeled in eastern areas of the species' range but may be slightly keeled in northeastern areas. The third, fourth, and fifth metacarpals are nearly equal. The skull is narrow with a long rostrum. The dental formula is i 2/3, c 1/1, p 3/3, m 3/3, total 38.

Biology, Life History, and Natural History

Reproductive Biology and Phenology

M. septentrionalis is polygamous. Breeding activity occurs in the fall and potentially extends into the spring. Initiation of swarming and breeding activities varies by geographic location, but, in general, these activities occur from late July in the northern part of the species' range to late August in the southern end of the range. Breeding activity extends into September and October. Histological data suggest that *M. septentrionalis* males behave in a manner similar to other North American vespertilionid bats in displaying testicular gametic function in summer followed by a regression of the gonads before mating and hibernation. Hibernating females store sperm in their uteruses until spring ovulation (Racey 1982). Females begin leaving hibernacula in March (southern areas) through May (northern areas), with maximum numbers leaving from late May to late June (south to north, respectively).

[1] Wildlife biologist, U.S. Department of Agriculture, Forest Service, North Central Research Station, Columbia, MO.
[2] Postdoctoral associate, Department of Fisheries and Wildlife Science, University of Missouri, Columbia, MO.

The gestation period, measured from implantation to parturition, is estimated at 50 to 60 days (Baker 1983). One pup born in late May (south) to July (north) is typical (Amelon 2001; Kunz 1971; Kurta 1980, 1982; Caire et al. 1979). Volant young have been observed as early as 3 weeks following parturition (Amelon 2001; Kunz 1971, 1973; Feldhammer et al. 2001). In Iowa and New Hampshire, subadults were captured as early as July (Clark and Rattner 1987, Sasse and Pekins 1996). Data available from the literature suggest that differences in maturity rates vary by geographical location of the population. Subadult *M. septentrionalis* have been observed at hibernacula in early August in Missouri (LaVal and LaVal 1980).

Ecology and Behavior

Comparisons of wing morphology with known habitat associations suggest that bats with low aspect ratios forage in the high clutter of forests while those with high aspect ratios forage in more open areas. The wings have an aspect ratio of 5.8 and wing loading of 6.8 (Norberg and Raynor 1987). The wingtip is very rounded. Each of these structural characteristics is consistent with bats that use a "gleaning" foraging strategy, which indicates they have adapted to foraging in canopy gaps and forested areas characterized by open understories and low density where the bats can capture prey items moving on foliage (Amelon 2001). Faure et al. (1993) found this species produces 1 millisecond frequency-modulated echolocation calls with a frequency range of 60 to 126 kilohertz and an intensity of 78 decibels at 10 centimeters, which is consistent with a bat using a gleaning foraging strategy (Fenton et al. 1983, Neuweiler 1989).

M. septentrionalis' winter and summer ranges were reported to be the same (Barbour and Davis 1969); however, the lack of hibernacula or reproductively active individuals suggests that portions of the population may move seasonally. Kurta (1982) suggested populations in areas of southern Michigan that have no caves or mines may move to southern areas of the range during the winter. An individual male captured in Missouri traveled 56 kilometers (km) in a month from a cave to an apparent summer location where it was recaptured behind a shutter on a house (Caire et al. 1979). Griffin (1940) reported an individual that moved at least 97 km between two caves between February and April.

Disproportionate sex ratios have been reported, suggesting geographic or habitat segregation. Kunz (1971) in Iowa and Grindal (1999) in Newfoundland found a 2:1 ratio of females to males in summer riparian habitat. Most of the males were captured in May and August, when they moved between winter and summer locations. In Arkansas, Wilhide et al. (1998) found a 1.2:1 ratio of females to males during trapping activities at upland ponds. Whitaker and Rissler (1992a) found a ratio of 1:1.2 females to males between November and March at a hibernacula in Indiana. Griffin (1945), Hitchcock (1949), Pearson and Barr (1962), and Stones (1981) found distribution of sexes at hibernacula to range from 60 to 78 percent males in hibernacula surveys. These authors suggested that females may have a higher mortality rate than males, but it seems equally feasible, based on high female ratios in summer habitat surveys that females may use less observable portions of hibernacula or different hibernacula from males.

In spring, *M. septentrionalis* disperses from hibernacula and migrates to maternity roosts. During the maternity period, sexes are segregated; females roost in small maternity colonies and males roost singly. Maternity colonies of 2 to 99 females have been reported (Burke 1999, Lacki and Ladeur 2001, Owen 2001, Menzel et al. 2000). Lactating females switch roost trees every 2 to 5 days (Foster and Kurta 1999, Lacki and Schwierjohann 2001, Owen 2001, Menzel et al. 2002). Individuals within the colony frequently may alternate their roost trees and association with other females of the group (Owen 2001, Sasse and Pekins 1996).

Obligate associations with other species have not been observed. *M. septentrionalis* has been observed in hibernacula with *M. lucifugus, M. sodalis, M. grisescens, M. leibii, Eptesicus fuscus,* and *Pipistrellus subflavus,* and they generally make up a small percentage of bats within a hibernacula (Graves and Harvey 1974, Hall 1981, Mumford and Cope 1964, Pearson and Barr 1962, Whitaker and Rissler 1992b, Caire et al. 1979).

Hibernation

Mammalian hibernation is characterized by periods of torpor interrupted cyclically by spontaneous arousal. Individuals aroused during hibernation tend to fly or move around between periods of torpor. *M. septentrionalis* appears to be an obligate hibernator. Caire et al. (1979) found prehibernation fat deposition of 41 to 45 percent with normal weights observed in the spring, which is consistent with fat deposition requirements of obligate hibernators. Hibernation occurs singly or in very small groups in caves and mines and potentially in crevices in hillsides or rock outcrops. Hibernating *M. septentrionalis* is usually found in crevices in the walls or ceilings of hibernacula (Caire et al. 1979, Whitaker and Gummer 2001).

Food Habits

This species is likely an opportunistic insectivore (Kunz 1973). Analysis of stomach contents and fecal pellets (Brack and Whitaker 2001) revealed that the diet of *M. septentrionalis* consists of species of lepidopterans, coleopterans, trichopterans, and dipterans. Prey items such as spiders and lepidopteran larvae made up 12.7 percent of the food found in the bats' stomachs, further supporting the gleaning foraging strategy of this species. In West Virginia, Carter et al. (2003) found diets of *M. septentrionalis* consisted of coleopterans and lepidopterans. In the Central Appalachians, Griffith and Gates (1985) found the species' diet consisted of lepidopterans, coleopterans, neuropterans, and dipterans.

Mortality and Predation Factors

Failure to store sufficient fat reserves may cause significant mortality among subadults during the first hibernation period (Davis and Reite 1967). No consistent predators were noted. Human disturbance and persecution at hibernacula may be significant in some locations. Ectoparasites include batbugs (*Cimex adjunctus*), chiggers (*Euschoengastia pipistrelli*), and mites (*Spinturax americanus*) (Sasse and Pekins 2000, Whitaker and Mumford 1973).

Longevity

Age structure is unknown. The highest longevity record for *M. septentrionalis* is an individual found dead in a cave 19 years after initial capture (Hall et al. 1957).

Banding Data

Banding information has been associated primarily with activities at the hibernacula. Hall and Brenner (1968) reported a 5.8-percent recapture rate for individuals that were banded during swarming activities and were subsequently found hibernating.

Site Fidelity

In homing experiments, Griffin (1945) found high return rates for bats released away from their capture site. One individual returned 51.5 km to its home cave in 2.5 hours after being held 3 days in captivity. Caire et al. (1979) banded 945 individuals at hibernacula in Missouri; 47 individuals (4.9 percent) were subsequently recaptured at the same hibernacula the following fall. Similarly, in Ohio, Mills (1971) recaptured 4.8 percent of 358 individuals at their cave of origin the year after initial capture.

Distribution

M. septentrionalis occurs throughout most of the Eastern United States and southern Canada (Hamilton and Whitaker 1979). The northern border of the range is Newfoundland, Quebec, and the Northwest Territories of Canada. The range extends southward along the East Coast to Florida and then westward through Alabama, Arkansas, and the eastern Great Plains (Hamilton and Whitaker 1979, van Zyll de Jong 1985, Harvey et al. 1991) (fig. 1). Although *M. septentrionalis* is widespread, its distribution may be irregular or patchy. It is more common in the northern part of its range than in the southern and western areas. This species is reported to be very

Figure 1. *The distribution of* Myotis septentrionalis.

* = Isolated or questionable records.

Source: Bat Conservation International 2003, http://www.batcon.org.

rare in Alabama (Best 2001) and uncommon in Kentucky, Tennessee, and Wisconsin (Mumford and Cope 1964, Hamilton and Whitaker 1979).

Habitat Requirements

Maternity Period (May to August)

Roosting Habitat
Maternity roosting sites vary by geographic location. Roost sites selected, regardless of geographic location, are warm sites that maximize growth rate of the young. Male roost sites and nonreproductive female summer roost sites may be found in cooler locations including caves and mines. Maternity colonies have been reported in tree cavities and crevices, under exfoliating bark, in live trees, and in expansion joints of bridges (Foster and Kurta 1999, Lacki and Ladeur 2001, Owen 2001, Feldhammer et al. 2003, Menzel et al. 2002). A colony of 99 females was reported using a "rocket box" type bat house. The preference of tree species depends on the geographic location. In Michigan, *M. septentrionalis* roosted in crevices, in hollows, or under the bark of maple (*Acer saccharinum*) and ash (*Fraxinus pennsylvanica*) (Foster and Kurta 1999).

In West Virginia, Owen (2001) found maternity roosts in cavities or under exfoliating bark in 11 tree species. Black locust (*Robinia pseudoacacia*) and black cherry (*Prunus serotina*) were used in higher proportions than availability of these species. The largest maternity colony (88 individuals) recorded in this study was observed exiting a cavity in a live black cherry tree. Additional tree species reported as *M. septentrionalis* maternity roost sites include elm (*Ulmus spp.*) (Clark et al. 1987), American beech (*Fagus grandifolia*) (Sasse and Pekins 1996), and sourwood (*Oxydendrum arboreum*) and shortleaf pine (*Pinus echinata*) (Lacki and Schwierjohann 2001). Lacki and Schwierjohann (2001) also found roosts to be associated with upper slopes and midslopes.

Foraging Habitat
M. septentrionalis typically occurs in forested habitats, in small openings, and occasionally over water. LaVal and Clawson (1977) observed 11 individuals foraging among trees along hillsides and ridges instead of riparian areas. In Iowa, Kunz (1971, 1973) found females that foraged in mature deciduous uplands and occasionally in adjacent floodplains and agricultural lands. Peak foraging occurs the first 2 hours after dusk and the last 2 hours before dawn.

Hibernation Period (October to April)
The use of different types of hibernacula varies geographically. Suitable conditions for hibernacula include high humidity, consistently low temperature, and lack of disturbance. Mines with temperatures of 7 to 9 °C in Michigan accounted for approximately 50 percent of the observed hibernating population (Andersen and Robert 1971). The species used caves, mines, and rock crevices as winter hibernation sites (Harvey et al. 1999a, 1999b). Whitaker and Rissler (1992b) observed *M. septentrionalis* using tiny cracks in the wall of an abandoned mine in Indiana. The difficulty in observing these bats in small crevices may in part explain the disparity between relatively high numbers of this species recorded in summer surveys and the low numbers recorded in hibernacula counts. Hibernation counts for this species rarely exceed 100 individuals.

Potential Threats

Natural or Human Factors
Factors contributing to population declines include flooding (Hall 1962); disturbance by humans and vandalism of hibernacula (Fenton 1970, Humphrey 1978, Speakman et al. 1991, Thomas 1993, Tuttle 1979); mine closures (Whitaker and Gummer 1992); and nursery roost removal. Disturbance during the hibernation or maternity periods is a significant factor in the widespread decline of cave- and mine- dependent bat species (Clark 1987, Currie 1999). Destruction of roost sites, particularly hibernacula, is the foremost factor leading to population declines (Humphrey 1978, Sheffield and Chapman 1992). North American bat conservation efforts have therefore focused primarily on protecting hibernacula from vandalism and physical alterations. Food chain poisoning by pesticides—in particular insecticides such as organochlorines and anticholinesterase—has been demonstrated to negatively impact insectivorous bats; these impacts may not result in death

but in impairment of productivity (Clark 1988, 2001; Clark and Krynitsky 1983; Cockrum 1970; Reidinger and Cockrum 1978). Colonies could be slow to recover because of low reproductive rates.

Present or Potential Risks to Habitat

Although much still has to be learned about the maternity and winter habitat requirements of this species, initial information on summer habitat indicate *M. septentrionalis* uses dead or damaged trees in landscapes that include upland hardwoods or pine-hardwood forest types. Because this habitat is widespread and abundant in eastern North America, the primary risk to habitat may be for wintering habitat or may involve pesticide exposure in summer habitats. The widespread recreational use of caves and indirect or direct disturbance by humans during the hibernation period pose the greatest known threat to this species. One major threat is the lack of knowledge about the species' life history needs and population status. Altering cave and mine microclimates by modifying air flow patterns may pose a threat to this species.

Inadequacy of Existing Regulatory Mechanisms

Early bat roost protection efforts focused on eliminating or reducing human disturbance during critical hibernation and maternity periods by installing informative signs or "bat friendly" gates and fences. In some cases, these efforts were unfavorable to bat populations because of changes in bat behavior and/or changes in cave microclimate factors due to construction activities. Protecting natural and human-made roosting structures is one of the highest priorities including maintaining water features associated with roosts. Funding to facilitate these protection measures is often unavailable. Hibernation counts to assess trends have not been consistent for this species.

Population Status

Rangewide

Both Global Heritage Status and National Heritage Status is "4," indicating the species is common (NatureServe 2002). Individual State Heritage Status is described in State Summaries and in table 1.

Table 1. *Population status of* Myotis septentrionalis *by State* [1].

State	Status[2]	Summer habitat	Winter habitat
Alabama	S2		
Arkansas	S2	Tree cavities, crevices, and under bark	Caves and mines
Connecticut	SNR/SU		
Delaware	SNR/SU		
Florida	SH		
Georgia	S3		
Illinois	S4		Caves and mines
Indiana	S3	Trees and buildings	
Iowa	S4	Trees	Caves and mines
Kansas	S2	Trees	Caves and mines
Kentucky	S4	Trees	Trees, caves, mines, and bridges
Maine	S4		
Maryland	S4		

Table 1. *Population status of* Myotis septentrionalis *by State* [1] *(continued).*

State	Status[2]	Summer habitat	Winter habitat
Massachusetts	S3		
Michigan	SNR/SU	Trees	Mines
Minnesota	S3		
Mississippi	S3		
Missouri	S3	Tree cavities, crevices, and under bark	Caves and mines
Montana	S2		
Nebraska	S3		
New Hampshire	S3		
New Jersey	SNR/SU		
New York	S3		
North Carolina	S3	Trees	Caves
North Dakota	SNR/SU		
Ohio	SNR/SU		
Oklahoma	S2	Trees	
Pennsylvania	S3		Caves
Rhode Island	S2		
South Carolina	S4	Trees	
South Dakota	S3		
Tennessee	S4		
Vermont	S4		
Virginia	S3		
West Virginia	S3		
Wisconsin	S4		

[1] Information about population and habitat use is based on literature cited. See text and References section.

[2] Status based on Natural Heritage State Rarity ranks (NatureServe 2002). S2: Very rare; usually between 5 and 20 occurrences, or, in the case of communities, covering less than 250 hectares in aggregate; or few occurrences with many individuals; often susceptible to becoming endangered. S3: Rare to uncommon; usually between 20 and 100 occurrences; may have fewer occurrences, but with a large number of individuals in some populations; may be susceptible to large-scale disturbances. S4: Common; usually more than 100 occurrences, but may be fewer with many large populations; may be restricted to only a portion of the State; usually not susceptible to immediate threats. SH: Historically known from the State, but not verified for an extended period (usually more than 15 years); this rank is used primarily when inventory has been attempted recently. SNR/SU: Status not ranked/Status uncertain, often because of low search effort or cryptic nature of the element.

Habitat Status

Summary of Land Ownership and Existing Habitat Protection

National Forests

Estimates of the potential available habitat for *M. septentrionalis*, were based on U.S. Department of Agriculture (USDA) Forest Service, Forest Inventory and Analysis (FIA) data, which estimates the amount of upland hardwood and pine-hardwood forest land more than 60 years old for all States with national forests in Regions 8 and 9 (Southern and Eastern Forest Service Regions combined to look at the entire species range) and Region 9 (examined alone to look at potential available habitat for States in the Eastern Region), excluding rarely used deciduous forest types such as aspen. This coarse-scale assessment of habitat availability considers forest type and age class based on USDA Forest Service FIA data (USDA Forest Service 2003); this analysis does not consider other aspects of forest structure that may influence use by this species. The database used is subject to sampling errors associated with coarse-scale inventory. Estimates were for the acreage of upland hardwood and pine-hardwood forest land for forests of all ownerships, including other federally owned, State-owned, county/municipal-owned, and privately owned lands within these States. Approximately 5.9 percent of upland hardwood, bottom-land hardwood, and pine-hardwood forest types occur on National Forest System (NFS) lands within the eastern range of this species; 2.9 percent occur on NFS lands within Region 9 (figs. 2 and 5). Estimates indicate that 358,219,772 acres of upland hardwood, bottom-land hardwood, and pine-hardwood forest land could potentially serve as foraging habitat occur within the eastern range of this species. Estimates also indicate that stands more than 60 years old in upland hardwood and pine-hardwood forest types would provide suitable trees to meet the roosting requirements of this species. Within the eastern range of *M. septentrionalis*, estimates indicate that 330,457,331 acres occur, and 88,687,204 acres, or 27 percent of the total available, is more than 60 years old (figs. 3 and 4). On NFS lands within Region 9, estimates indicate 9,671,251 acres of potential foraging habitat (upland hardwood, bottom-land hardwood, and pine-hardwood forest

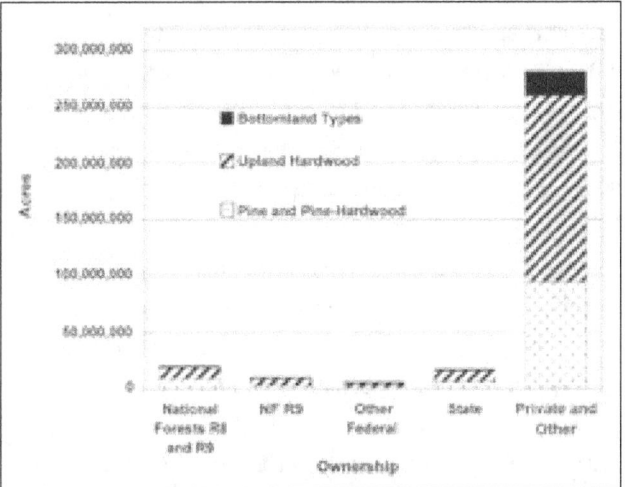

Figure 2. *Ownership of upland hardwood, bottom-land hardwood, and pine-hardwood forest types within States overlapping the range of* M. septentrionalis.

Alabama, Arkansas, Connecticut, Delaware, Florida, Georgia, Illinois, Indiana, Iowa, Kansas, Kentucky, Maine, Maryland, Massachusetts, Michigan, Minnesota, Mississippi, Missouri, Montana, Nebraska, New Hampshire, New Jersey, New York, North Carolina, North Dakota, Ohio, Oklahoma, Pennsylvania, Rhode Island, South Carolina, South Dakota, Tennessee, Vermont, Virginia, West Virginia, Wisconsin.

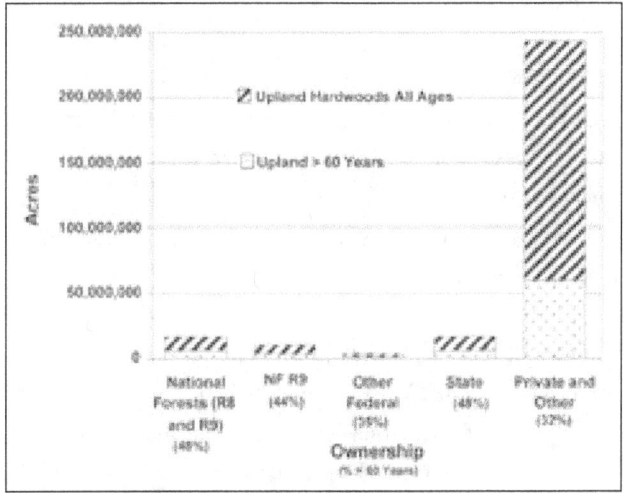

Figure 3. *Acreage by ownership of upland hardwood forest type and percentage of upland hardwood forest type more than 60 years old by ownership within States overlapping the range of* M. septentrionalis.

Alabama, Arkansas, Connecticut, Delaware, Florida, Georgia, Illinois, Indiana, Iowa, Kansas, Kentucky, Maine, Maryland, Massachusetts, Michigan, Minnesota, Mississippi, Missouri, Montana, Nebraska, New Hampshire, New Jersey, New York, North Carolina, North Dakota, Ohio, Oklahoma, Pennsylvania, Rhode Island, South Carolina, South Dakota, Tennessee, Vermont, Virginia, West Virginia, Wisconsin.

Figure 4. *Acreage by ownership of pine and pine-hardwood forest types and percentage of pine and pine-hardwood forest types more than 60 years old by ownership within States overlapping the range of* M. septentrionalis.

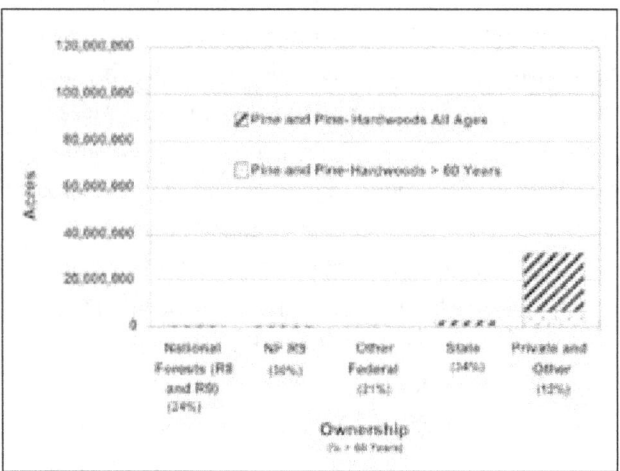

Alabama, Arkansas, Connecticut, Delaware, Florida, Georgia, Illinois, Indiana, Iowa, Kansas, Kentucky, Maine, Maryland, Massachusetts, Michigan, Minnesota, Mississippi, Missouri, Montana, Nebraska, New Hampshire, New Jersey, New York, North Carolina, North Dakota, Ohio, Oklahoma, Pennsylvania, Rhode Island, South Carolina, South Dakota, Tennessee, Vermont, Virginia, West Virginia, Wisconsin.

Figure 5. *Acreage by ownership of bottom-land hardwood forest type and percentage of bottom-land hardwood forest type more than 60 years old by ownership within States overlapping the range of* M. septentrionalis.

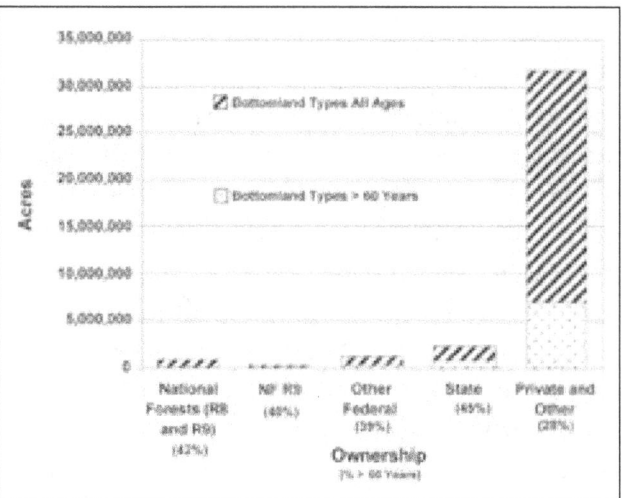

Alabama, Arkansas, Florida, Georgia, Illinois, Indiana, Kentucky, Louisiana, Mississippi, Missouri, North Carolina, Oklahoma, South Carolina, Tennessee, Texas, Virginia.

types) and 3,786,768 acres of upland hardwood and pine-hardwood forest types more than 60 years old (40.3 percent) are available for roosting (figs. 3 and 4).

State Summaries

Illinois. State status is common (S4, table 1). In a study on the Shawnee National Forest that looked at 71 potential hibernation sites at caves and mines, mines were found to be the only sites used by *M. septentrionalis* (Whitaker and Winter 1977). Pearson and Barr (1962) found that 72 percent of individuals hibernating at silica mines were male.

Indiana. State status is rare to uncommon (S3, table 1). Whitaker et al. (2002) assessed population levels over time of 10 species of bats in Indiana and found populations of *M. septentrionalis* to be relatively low but stable between 1980 and 2000. Whitaker and Stacy (1996) found *M. septentrionalis* at 5 of 13 abandoned coal mines that contained bats; this species accounted for 39 percent of the bats captured.

Michigan. State status is undetermined (SNR/SU, table 1). Up to 60 female *M. septentrionalis* in Michigan roosted in large-diameter, live or dead maple and ash trees (Foster and Kurta 1999). Individuals switched roosts frequently, and roost trees were clustered in a 20-hectare (ha) site. No significant differences were found between occupied and unoccupied roosts. Stones (1981) found more than 100 individuals in 5 of 21 mines surveyed. This species accounted for approximately 60 percent of winter population counts.

Minnesota. State status is rare to uncommon (S3, table 1). Goehring (1954) reported several *M. septentrionalis* bats hibernating in shallow crevices of a storm sewer with high relative humidity and temperatures ranging from 1.7 to 6.7 °C.

Missouri. State status is rare to uncommon (S3, table 1). The distribution and activity of bats on the Mark Twain National Forest were studied in the summer and fall between 1997 and 2003. Surveys sampled upland flyways and ponds and riparian areas; *M. septentrionalis* accounted for 28 to 36 percent of bats captured each year. Both males (71 percent of captures) and females (59 percent of captures) were captured most frequently at upland ponds in summer. Streams accounted for 17 percent of male captures and 22 percent of female captures; flyways and trails accounted for 12 percent of male captures and 13 percent of female captures. Fall captures in uplands and riparian areas represented only 5 percent of total captures (Amelon 2001).

New Hampshire. State status is rare to uncommon (S3, table 1). The summer roosting ecology of female *M. septentrionalis* was studied on the White Mountain National Forest (Sasse and Pekins 1996). Of 281 bats captured during the study, *M. septentrionalis* represented 27 percent of the captures and *M. lucifugus* represented 71 percent. Of the *M. septentrionalis* bats, 26 were tracked to 47 roost trees; 66 percent of the roosts were beech and maple snags. Bats in this study switched roosts frequently. Roosts were occupied by a mean colony size of 11 bats during pregnancy. There was no difference in colony sizes using live versus dead trees; however, 5 of 7 roosts with more than 24 bats were in snags. Snags used as roosts had larger diameters, more bark, and lower stand canopy closure than did random snags. Sasse and Pekins (1996) suggested that snag characteristics alone may not adequately describe roost characteristics because this species roosted in locations with higher mean live-tree diameters.

Krusic et al. (1996) used ultrasonic detectors to survey the bat species' flight activity in forests of varying age structure within the White Mountain National Forest. In this study, calls of Myotis species were grouped, and it would therefore be difficult to draw any inferences relative to the use of these habitats by *M. septentrionalis*. In addition, it has been shown that bat echolocation calls are strongly affected by the amount of clutter in the vicinity of the recorder. Bat echolocation calls are also affected by relatively small differences in temperature and relative humidity (Hayes 2000, Hayes and Gruver 2000, Livengood 2001). These limitations make it difficult to draw inferences about relative activity between habitat types or age classes without simultaneously accounting for differences in the size of sampled areas and differences in sound intensity between echolocation calls of different species.

Ohio. State status is undetermined (SNR/SU, table 1). The distribution and activity of bats on the Wayne National Forest were studied in the summer and winter of 1979 and 1980. Surveys were conducted at abandoned mines and riparian sites; *M. septentrionalis* was found hibernating in 23 of 65 coal mine shafts. *M. septentrionalis* accounted for less than 4 percent of the bats captured in summer surveys of riparian areas (Lacki and Bookhout 1983).

Pennsylvania. State status is rare to uncommon (S3, table 1). An analysis of mammals in Pennsylvania based on population status, habitat, and threats ranked *M. septentrionalis* as rare (Kirkland and Krim 1990). Between 1980 and 1988, 190 caves and abandoned mines were surveyed for bats. Hibernating bats were found at 135 sites, or 71 percent of the sites; *M. septentrionalis* was found at 34 of these locations (Kirkland and Krim 1990).

Hall and Brenner (1968) found peak swarming activity occurred in mid-August. Males accounted for approximately 81 percent of the captures.

Vermont. State status is common (S4, table 1). In surveys conducted in 1999 and 2000 on the Green Mountain National Forest, *M. septentrionalis* was the most commonly captured species (Reynolds 2000, Amelon et al. 2000). This species was captured at three of five locations along trails and roads in 2000. In 1999, *M. septentrionalis* was captured at 9 of 10 locations. Of the 40 individuals caught in August, 26 were caught near hibernacula, 8 were caught over streams, and 1 was caught along a logging trail. Griffin (1940) found 78 percent individuals noted in hibernacula counts were male.

West Virginia. State status is rare to common (S3, table 1). Of 159 bats captured by Carter et al. (2003) in the Allegheny Plateau and the Ridge and Valley physiographic province, 40 were members of *M. septentrionalis* (25 percent). The foraging area of 7 females averaged 61.1 ha (Menzel 1999).

Wisconsin. State status is common (S4, table 1). An abandoned mine in southeastern Wisconsin contained approximately 1,000 *M. septentrionalis* among 77,000 bats that included three other species. Males began arriving at the mine in July, and females began arriving in mid-August. Females were no longer detected after mid-October. Overall, males accounted for 60 percent of the captures at all sampling times. Spring departure began in late April; females left before males did.

References

Amelon, S.K. 2001. Unpublished data. Columbia, MO: U.S. Department of Agriculture, Forest Service, North Central Research Station.

Amelon, S.K.; Thompson, F.R.; Dijak, W.D. 2000. Habitat use and roost selection of forest bats on the Mark Twain National Forest, Missouri. Bat Research News. 41: 106.

Andersen, J.E.; Robert, C.S. 1971. A new unipolar electrode for electrocardiography in small mammals. Journal of Mammalogy. 52: 469-471.

Baker, M.D. 1983. Michigan mammals. Lansing, MI: University of Michigan. 344 p.

Barbour, R.W.; Davis, W.H. 1969. Bats of America. Lexington, KY: University of Kentucky Press. 286 p.

Best, T.L. 2001. Personal communication. Professor, Department of Zoology and Wildlife Science, Auburn University, Auburn, AL. Conversation.

Brack, V.; Whitaker, J.O. 2001. Foods of the northern myotis, *Myotis septentrionalis,* from Missouri and Indiana, with notes on foraging. Acta Chiropterologica. 3(2): 203-210.

Burke, H.S.J. 1999. Maternity colony formation in *Myotis septentrionalis* using artificial roosts: The rocket box, a habitat enhancement for woodland bats? Bat Research News. 40(3): 77-78.

Caceres, M.C.; Barclay, R.M.R. 2000. *Myotis septentrionalis.* Mammalian Species. 634: 1-3.

Caire, W.; LaVal, R.K.; LaVal, M.L.; Clawson, R. 1979. Note on the ecology of *Myotis keenii* in Eastern Missouri. American Midland Naturalist. 102: 404-407.

Carter, T.C.; Menzel, M.A.; Edwards, J.W.; Sheldon, O.F.; Menzel, J.M.; Ford, W.M. 2003. Food habits of seven species of bats in the Allegheny Plateau and Ridge and Valley of West Virginia. Northeast Naturalist. 10: 83-88.

Clark, D.R. 1987. Selenium accumulation in mammals exposed to contaminated California irrigation drainwater. The Science of the Total Environment. 66: 147-168.

Clark, D.R.; Rattner, B.A. 1987. Orthene toxicity to little brown bats (*Myotis lucifugus*): acetylcholinesterase inhibition, coordination loss, and mortality. Environmental Toxicology and Chemistry. 6: 705-708.

Clark, D.R., Jr. 1988. Environmental contaminants and the management of bat populations in the United States. In: Proceedings, Symposium on management of amphibians, reptiles, and small mammals in North America. Laurel, MD: U.S. Fish & Wildlife Service: 409-413.

Clark, D.R., Jr. 2001. DDT and the decline of free-tailed bats (*Tadarida brasiliensis*) at Carlsbad Caverns, New Mexico. Archives of Environmental Contamination and Toxicology. 40: 537-543.

Clark, D.R., Jr.; Krynitsky, A.J. 1983. DDE in brown and white fat of hibernating bats. Environmental Toxicology and Chemistry. 31: 287-299.

Cockrum, E.L. 1970. Insecticides and guano bats. Ecology. 51: 761-762.

Currie, R.R. 1999. An overview of the response of bats to protection efforts. In: Proceedings, Indiana Bat Symposium. Lexington, KY: Bat Conservation International. 24 p.

Davis, W.H.; Reite, O.B. 1967. Responses of bats from temperate regions to changes in ambient temperature. Biological Bulletin. 132: 320-328.

Faure, P.A.; Fullard, J.H.; Dawson, J.W. 1993. The gleaning attacks of the northern long-eared bat, *Myotis septentrionalis*, are relatively inaudible to moths. Journal of Experimental Biology. 178: 173-189.

Feldhammer, G.A.; Carter, T.C.; Carroll, S.K. 2001. Timing of pregnancy, lactation and female foraging activity in three species of bats in southern Illinois. Canadian Field-Naturalist. 115(3): 420-424.

Feldhammer, G.A.; Carter, T.C.; Nicholson, E.H.; Morzillo, A.T. 2003. Use of bridges as day roosts by bats in southern Illinois. Transactions, Illinois State Academy Science. 96: 107-112.

Fenton, M.B. 1970. Population studies of *Myotis lucifugus* in Ontario. Life Sci. Occas. Pap. Toronto, ON: Royal Ontario Museum. 77: 1-34.

Fenton, M.B.; Merriam, H.G.; Holroyd, G.L. 1983. Bats of Kootenay, Glacier and Mount Revelstoke National Parks in Canada: identification by echolocation calls, distribution and biology. Canadian Journal of Zoology. 61: 2503-2508.

Foster, R.W.; Kurta, A. 1999. Roosting ecology of the northern bat (*Myotis septentrionalis*) and comparisons with the endangered Indiana bat (*Myotis sodalis*). Journal of Mammalogy. 80(2): 659-672.

Goehring, A.B. 1954. *Pipistrellus subflavus, Myotis keenii,* and *Eptesicus fuscus* hibernating in a storm sewer in central Minnesota. Journal of Mammalogy. 35: 434-435.

Graves, F.F.; Harvey, M.J. 1974. Distribution of Chiroptera in western Tennessee. Journal of the Tennessee Academy of Science. 49(3): 106-109.

Griffin, D.R. 1940. Notes on the life histories of New England cave bats. Journal of Mammalogy. 21: 181-187.

Griffin, D.R. 1945. Travels of banded cave bats. Journal of Mammalogy. 26: 15-23.

Griffith, L.A.; Gates, J.E. 1985. Food habits of cave-dwelling bats in the central Appalachians. Journal of Mammalogy. 66(3): 451-460.

Grindal, S.D. 1999. Habitat use by bats, *Myotis* spp., in western Newfoundland. Canadian Field Naturalist. 113(2): 258-263.

Hall, E.R. 1981. The mammals of North America. New York: John Wiley & Sons. 600 p.

Hall, J.S. 1962. A life history and taxonomic study of the Indiana bat, *Myotis sodalis*. Reading Public Museum and Art Gallery, Science Publication. 12: 1-68.

Hall, J.S.; Brenner, F.J. 1968. Summer netting of bats at a cave in Pennsylvania. Journal of Mammalogy. 49: 779-781.

Hall, J.S.; Cloutier, R.J.; Griffin, D.R. 1957. Longevity records and notes on tooth wear of bats. Journal of Mammalogy. 38: 407-409.

Hamilton, W.J.; Whitaker, J.O., Jr. 1979. Mammals of the Eastern United States. Ithaca, NY: Cornell University Press. 346 p.

Harvey, M.J.; Altenback, J.S.; Best, T.L. 1999a. Bats of the United States. Little Rock, AR: Arkansas Game and Fish Commission. 64 p.

Harvey, M.J.; MacGregor, J.R.; Currie, R.R. 1991. Distribution and status of Chiroptera in Kentucky and Tennessee. Journal of the Tennessee Academy of Science. 4: 191-193.

Harvey, M.J.; McDaniel, V.R.; Wilhide, J.D. 1999b. Behavioral ecology of endangered bats in Arkansas, 1993-1999. Little Rock, AR: Arkansas Game and Fish Commission. 118 p.

Hayes, J.P. 2000. Assumptions and practical considerations in the design and interpretation of echolocation-monitoring studies. Acta Chiropterologica. 2(2): 225-236.

Hayes, J.P.; Gruver, J.C. 2000. Vertical stratification of bat activity in an old-growth forest in western Washington. Northwest Science. 74(2): 102-108.

Hitchcock, H.B. 1949. Hibernation of bats in southeastern Ontario and adjacent Quebec. Canadian Field-Naturalist. 63: 47-59.

Humphrey, S.R. 1978. Status, winter habitat, and management of the endangered Indiana bat, *Myotis sodalis*. Florida Scientist. 41: 65-76.

Kirkland, G.L., Jr.; Krim, P.M. 1990. Survey of the status of the mammals of Pennsylvania. Journal of the Pennsylvania Academy of Science. 64(1): 33-45.

Krusic, R.A.; Yamasaki, M.; Neefus, C.D.; Pekins, P.J. 1996. Bat habitat use in White Mountain National Forest. Journal of Wildlife Management. 60: 625-631.

Kunz, T.H. 1971. Reproduction of some Vespertilionid bats in central Iowa. American Midland Naturalist. 86: 477-486.

Kunz, T.H. 1973. Resource utilization: temporal and spatial components of bat activity in central Iowa. Journal of Mammalogy. 54: 14-32.

Kurta, A. 1980. Status of the Indiana bat, *Myotis sodalis*, in Michigan. Michigan Academician. 13: 31-36.

Kurta, A. 1982. A review of Michigan bats: seasonal and geographic distribution. Michigan Academy of Science. 14: 295-312.

Lacki, M.J.; Bookhout, T.A. 1983. A survey of bats in Wayne National Forest, Ohio. Ohio Journal of Science. 83(1): 45-50.

Lacki, M.J.; Ladeur, K.M. 2001. Seasonal use of lepidopteran prey by Rafinesque's big-eared bats (*Corynorhinus rafinesquii*). American Midland Naturalist. 145: 213-217.

Lacki, M.J.; Schwierjohann, J.H. 2001. Day-roost characteristics of northern bats in mixed mesophytic forest. Journal of Wildlife Management. 65: 482-488.

LaVal, R.K.; Clawson, R.L. 1977. Foraging behavior and nocturnal activity patterns of Missouri bats, with emphasis on the endangered species *Myotis grisescens* and *Myotis sodalis*. Journal of Mammalogy. 58(4): 592-599.

LaVal, R.K.; LaVal, M.L. 1980. Ecological studies and management of Missouri bats, with emphasis on cave-dwelling species. Missouri Department of Conservation, Terrestrial Series. 8: 19.

Livengood, K. 2001. Personal communication. Graduate student, Department of Fisheries and Wildlife, University of Missouri, Columbia, MO. Conversation.

Manning, R.W. 1993. Systematic and evolutionary relationships of the long-eared myotis, *Myotis evotis* (Chiroptera: Vespertilionidae). Spec. Publ. The Museum, Texas Tech University. 37: 21186.

Menzel, M.A.; Carter, T.C.; Ford, W.M.; Chapman, B.R.; Ozier, J. 2000. Summer roost tree selection by eastern red, Seminole, and evening bats in the Upper Coast Plain of South Carolina. 54: 304-313.

Menzel, M.A.; Krishon, D.M.; Laerm, J.; Carter, T.C. 1999. Notes on tree roost characteristics of the northern yellow bat (*Lasiurus intermedius*), the Seminole bat (*L. seminolus*), and the eastern pipistrelle (*Pipistrellus subflavus*). Florida Scientist. 62: 185-193.

Menzel, M.A.; Menzel, J.A.; Castleberry, S.B.; Ozier, J.; Ford, W.M. 2002. Illustrated key to skins and skulls of bats in the Southeastern and Mid-Atlantic States. 9 p.

Miller, G.S.; Allen, G.M. 1928. The American bats of the genera *Myotis* and *Pizonyx*. Bulletin of the United States National Museum. 144: 1-218.

Mills, R.S. 1971. A concentration of *Myotis keenii* at caves in Ohio. Journal of Mammalogy. 52: 625.

Mumford, R.E.; Cope, J.B. 1964. Distribution and status of the Chiroptera of Indiana. American Midland Naturalist. 72(2): 473-489.

Nagorsen, D.W.; Brigham, R.M. 1993. Bats of British Columbia: Royal British Columbia museum handbook. Vancouver, Canada: University of British Columbia Press.

NatureServe. 2002. NatureServe Explorer: an online encyclopedia of life [Web application]. Version 4.1. http://www.natureserve.org.

Neuweiler, G. 1989. Foraging ecology and audition in echolocating bats. TREE. 4(6): 160-166.

Norberg, U.M.; Raynor, J.M.V. 1987. Ecological morphology and flight in bats (Mammalia: Chiroptera): wing adaptations, flight performance, foraging strategy and echolocation. Philosophical Transactions, Royal Society of London. 316: 335-427.

Owen, S. 2001. Homerange size and habitat use of the northern long-eared myotis (*Myotis septentrionalis*) in an industrial forest landscape in the Central Appalachian Mountains. http://www.nrac.wvu.edu/rm493-591/fall2000/students/owen.

Pearson, E.W.; Barr, T.R.B. 1962. Absence of rabies in some bats and shrews from southern Illinois. Illinois Academy of Science Transactions. 55: 5-37.

Racey, P.A. 1982. Ecology of bat reproduction. In: Kunz, T.H., ed. Ecology of bats. New York, NY: Plenum: 57-104.

Reidinger, R.F., Jr.; Cockrum, E.L. 1978. Organochlorine residues in free-tailed bats (*Tadarida brasiliensis*) at Eagle Creek Cave, Greenlee County, Arizona. In: Proceedings, Fourth International Bat Research Conference. Nairobi, Kenya: Kenya Literature Bureau: 85-96.

Reynolds, D.S. 2000. Woodland bat survey, Green Mountain National Forest. 17 p.

Sasse, D.B.; Pekins, P.J. 1996. Summer roosting ecology of northern long-eared bats (*Myotis septentrionalis*) in the White Mountain National Forest. Bats and forests symposium. British Columbia Ministry of Forests Working Paper. 23: 91-101.

Sasse, D.B.; Pekins, P.J. 2000. Ectoparasites observed on northern long-eared bats, *Myotis septentrionalis*. Bat Research News. 41(3): 69-71.

Sheffield, S.R.; Chapman, B.R. 1992. First records of mammals from McCurtain County, Oklahoma. Texas Journal of Science. 44: 491-492.

Speakman, J.; Racey, P.A.; Webb, P.I.; Catto, C.M.C.; Swift, S.M.; Burnett, A.M. 1991. Minimum summer populations and densities of bats in N.E. Scotland, near the northern borders of their distributions. Journal Zoology London. 225: 327-345.

Stones, R.C. 1981. Endangered and threatened species program: survey of winter bat populations in search of the Indiana bat in the western Upper Peninsula of Michigan. Michigan Department of Natural Resources.

Thomas, D.W. 1993. Lack of evidence for a biological alarm clock in bats (*Myotis* spp.): hibernating under natural conditions. Canadian Journal of Zoology. 71: 1-3.

Trouessart, E.L. 1897. Catalogus mammalium tam viventium quam follilium. In: Friedlaender, B.R.; Sohn; Nova, eds.: 1-664.

Tuttle, M.D. 1979. Status, causes of decline, and management of endangered gray bats. Journal of Wildlife Management. 43: 1-17.

U.S. Department of Agriculture, Forest Service. 2003. Forest Inventory and Analysis. 98 p.

van Zyll de Jong, C.G. 1979. Distribution and systematic relationships of long-eared myotis in western Canada. Canadian Journal of Zoology. 57: 987-994.

van Zyll de Jong, C.G. 1985. Handbook of Canadian mammals: bats. Ottawa: National Museums of Canada. 212 p. Vol. 2.

Whitaker, J.O.; Brack, J.V.; Cope, J.B. 2002. Are bats in Indiana declining? In: Proceedings, Indiana Academy of Science. 111: 95-106.

Whitaker, J.O.; Gummer, S.L. 1992. Hibernation of the big brown bat, *Eptesicus fuscus*, in buildings. Journal of Mammology. 73(2): 312-316.

Whitaker, J.O.; Gummer, S.L. 2001. Bats of the Wabash and Ohio River Basins of southwestern Indiana. In: Proceedings, Indiana Academy of Science. 110: 126-140.

Whitaker, J.O.; Mumford, R.E. 1973. External parasites of bats of Indiana. The Journal of Parasitology. 59: 1148-1150.

Whitaker, J.O.; Rissler, L.J. 1992a. Seasonal activity of bats at Copperhead Cave. In: Proceedings, Indiana Academy of Science. 101: 127-135.

Whitaker, J.O.; Rissler, L.J. 1992b. Winter activity of bats at a mine entrance in Vermillion County, Indiana. American Midland Naturalist. 127: 52-59.

Whitaker, J.O.; Stacy, M. 1996. Bats of abandoned coal mines in southwestern Indiana. In: Proceedings, Indiana Academy of Science. 105: 277-280.

Whitaker, J.O.; Winter, F.A. 1977. Bats of the caves and mines of the Shawnee National Forest, southern Illinois. Transactions Illinois Sta. Academy Science. 70: 301-313.

Wilhide, J.D.; McDaniel, V.R.; Harvey, M.J.; White, D.R. 1998. Telemetric observations of foraging Ozark big-eared bats in Arkansas. Journal of the Arkansas Academy of Science. 52: 113-115.

Williams, D.F.; Findley, J.S. 1979. Sexual size dimorphism in vespertilionid bats. The American Midland Naturalist. 102: 113-126.